IMPOSSIBLE
HILL

BY PETER TAUNTON

Discover Your Unstoppable Fire,
Destroy Your Limits and
Take The Hill Of Your Dreams.

D1248512

Dedication

Life has taught me that a man cannot separate himself from his story, for our stories are the legacies we leave behind and the crafting of them is what propel us towards the future. While there are too many stories interwoven into the tapestry of my life, my entire life story would make no sense without my three beautiful children who are and will remain the joy and legacy of my life. They continue to drive me to improve into a better version of myself and I love them deeply.

Sunny, as your name connotes, you are true warmth and light in my life.

Beau you are courageous and when I see you, I recognize the beauty of unlimited potential.

Max you are a visionary and I'm certain you'll maximize your ability to be a great leader.

I am proud of all three of you and I pray that God will always guide your steps.

Father, you've always been a steady role model for me, not only in business but in how you showed compassion for those less fortunate. You taught me resolve and honor and for that I am ever grateful.

My dear twin brother Paul, you've been a friend and competitor, a natural source of inspiration and we've pushed each other to be better in multiple ways. I am honored that God chose for us to share the journey of life together, with the ups and downs, I am grateful for your life. Even as small boys we pushed each other to the top of many mountains. There is joy in the hindsight of the struggle. I'm certain that the view from up top is made more special because we get to remember how we overcame our past challenges on the upward trek and now we get to see an even better future, together.

I want to acknowledge all of the incredible people I had the opportunity to work with over the thirty years of my business career, although I was the face of my brands I couldn't have accomplished this without their discipline, accountability and sacrifices they made to enabled us to make our dreams a reality. I want to thank you for your trust along the journey. There is an African proverb that says: "if you want to go fast, go alone. If you want to get far, go together." I'm grateful, because together we have indeed come far.

To the reader, may these words encourage you on your path and may my story help to push you further, climb higher and enact your best vision for your life.

Peter Taunton

Foreword

One of my earliest memories is one that I wish never happened. The fateful day started like any other day in a family with a 28-year-old mother and her 3 young boys. At 3 years old, I was the oldest child. I woke up excited, because my dad, US Army Captain Thomas McCarthy, who had been serving in Vietnam for 11 months was set to return home in a couple of weeks. That morning, as my Mom was helping my younger brothers get dressed, I looked out the window of the bedroom I shared with my brothers and saw a taxicab pull up to our driveway. An Army officer got out and began walking to our front door. I screamed to my Mom, "Dad is home!" She came to the window and saw the scene a wife of a soldier never wants to see. The Army officer was not my Dad. He was a soldier being sent by the Army to inform my Mom that my Dad had been killed in Vietnam the previous day. My mother made us stay in our room as she went to answer the door, but I still remember the scream she let out when her worst fear was confirmed. A few minutes later, the neighbors were in our home taking care of me and my little brothers and I could hear my Mom in another room crying for a long time.

The trajectory of my life would be forever altered. My Mom, who never remarried, devoted her life to raising her 3 young boys. We struggled financially and as I grew older, I could feel the almost daily pain and worry my mother was experiencing. It bothered me to see my Mom struggle to pay bills, put food on the table and take care of 3 young boys. Even though I was just a child, I was determined to find a way out of this situation for my family. Growing up in an Army family, I didn't have any role models for success in business, but for some reason, I had an innate entrepreneurial spirit. I was always starting businesses. At age 13 I had a citywide lawn mowing service for residential homes and commercial buildings with 3 employees. I had additional businesses where around the holidays I would climb trees to pick mistletoe and then sell it to the florists and in high school I would go to a hammock factory in a neighboring state to buy hammocks that we would sell in my city for a significant profit. I was also extremely fortunate to have a mentor, Mr. Bob Woodberry, who had been a good friend of my Dad's in the Army. Mr. Woodberry had gotten out of the Army after his 4-year commitment and had become extremely successful in the investment industry. He was my model for success, and I soaked in his wisdom and knowledge. His father had also passed away when Bob was young and his family had financial struggles, but after graduating from Dartmouth and serving in the Army, he had become one of the most prominent leaders in his industry.

Mr. Woodberry was incredibly generous with his time and knowledge and I would not be where I am today without his care and guidance. After college, I spent 3 years with a Wall Street firm followed by another 3 years as the Worldwide Head of Sales and Marketing for another mentor of mine, Tony

Robbins. After helping to grow Tony's company over 100% each year I was there, I decided it was time to start my own company. With big aspirations I created a company focused on providing leadership, communication and peak performance training and coaching for the corporate world. I wish I could tell you it was an overnight success, and everything turned out exactly as I planned, but that would be the furthest from the truth. It was a struggle and it felt to me like what Peter Taunton calls an Impossible Hill. There were times where I didn't know if I was going to make it, but looking back, the formula that Peter outlines in this book is the same strategy I followed to conquer my Impossible Hill. 1. Solidify Your Decision. 2. Clarify Your Vision. 3. Apply Constant Action.

My training company has grown to serve several of the largest companies in the world like Microsoft, Cisco Systems, Salesforce, Wells Fargo, AIG and Met Life. In addition, I have either started up or created ownership stakes in a chain of 19 healthy restaurants, a 3,000-agent insurance agency, a security software company, a hotel on Waikiki beach, a CBD manufacturing business, 120,000 acres of ranch land in Arizona and a real estate portfolio of shopping centers, apartment complex, industrial buildings and single-family homes across the US and Europe. All of this success and the millions of dollars I have earned over the years came from the principles that Peter will share with you in this book.

While I had my personal mentor in Mr. Woodberry, this book provides you with an incredible mentor in Peter. I have worked with thousands of leaders over the past 30 years, but very few have come anywhere close to achieving the success that Peter has produced in his career. Growing up in a small town and going to school in a two-room schoolhouse, Peter, just like me, lacked role models of success in business. But that was never going to stop him. His competitive desire led him to become one of the top racquetball players in the country and also led him to take on the challenge of turning around a failing fitness club. In a few short years, Peter not only climbed the hill of making the club profitable, he acquired an ownership stake in the club and then expanded from one club into several clubs. That was only the beginning. Eventually his Hill Taking strategy led him to being able to create one of the largest fitness and wellness companies in the world with over 6,000 locations, spread across multiple brands in 28 countries. Many people can talk about their philosophy of success, but few have truly lived it the way Peter has. In choosing a mentor, I always look for someone who has actually done what they are talking about. With Peter, rest assured, you have the mentor who will give you the straight story and provide you with a blueprint you can use time after time to overtake your Impossible Hills.

I'm excited that Peter has committed to helping you by taking the time to write this book. Not only is Peter an absolute authority on how to create and run a successful business, he is also an outstanding human being that I am proud to call my friend. If you follow the wisdom that will unfold when you read this book, I have 100% confidence that years from now you will be able to look back and thank Peter for the tremendous success he helped you create.

Keep Living Your Dreams!

Tom McCarthy

Table of Contents

Chapter 1

UNSTOPPABLE FIRE

No matter a person's social status or income, whether the economy is booming or surging. It's the select few people who take the hill head on who seem to win in all conditions. I have always been fascinated with the people in this world that have gone before me, who have left an example for us to follow. For me, I remember where this part of myself first began showing up in my life.

When I sat down to create the ideas I would write in this book; it occurred to me that my father was the first example I had of what it means to be a hilltaker. Looking back on my 35-year career in business, he set the principles that I used to start my first business at eight years old. Little did I know; those were the same principles that helped me start the international fitness franchise, Snap Fitness.

Even to this day, as I share this message, I still remember the day my father sat the family down and told us that we were moving. I was four years old at the time and as the youngest of 7 children living in Minneapolis. I went to school in a two-room schoolhouse and shared a bedroom with my two brothers. We had no carpet, and I will never forget the nails poking holes in the unfinished ceiling. I remember those days fondly and can still picture the cowboy light fixture in my room. The symbolism of that cowboy would become a fixture for the entire Taunton family.

My father wanted better for us, and he was willing to risk everything to make sure we had a better life. At that time, a move from Minneapolis to Willmar, Minnesota, was considered a loss instead of an opportunity. Willmar had a population of 15,000, but my father saw the potential. It was time to cowboy up, and we were all along for the ride.

He had taken over the local Red Owl Grocery store, and although I didn't see it, it was that moment that would define my life forever. The Red Owl was failing when my father arrived, but he was determined to change it. It was his ambition and attitude that inspired me the most. He was always one of the first ones to the store and one of the last ones to close up shop. Six days per week, my father worked tirelessly, but you could never tell by his attitude.

My father was quick to greet everyone with a smile and a handshake. He would be bagging groceries, running the checkout stand, and stocking the shelves. My father put himself above nothing and above no one. That work ethic resonates with most people today, and it resonated with people back then as well. I saw the determination in his work ethic. Failure was not an option, and there was no plan B. He did, however, close on Sundays because Sunday was reserved for family and church.

This is where I first learned the full meaning of showing up and taking the hill. My father risked everything to create a better life for our family and worked tirelessly to make sure that was a reality. Still, he never forgot to take the hill with his family, and he showed up for the people who counted on him.

By the age of 8, my father let me start helping out at the store. Eager to show what I had learned by watching him, I started a popcorn stand, my first successful business. Every day I saw my father leading by example. He had an unstoppable fire. I learned work ethic, intentionality, and compassion for everyone, even for those that may wrong you.

One day, as I walked by my father's office, I noticed a man sitting in a chair face to face with my dad. He was clearly in some sort of trouble, and I will never forget the look on my father's face. A few moments later, the guy left the store. Just as any curious 8-year-old would, I asked him what happened. My father explained, the man had sewn pockets along the inside lining of his jacket and was caught filling those pockets with steaks. Sure of the answer I would receive, I asked him if he called the police.

"No, Son, I gave him the steaks."

Dumbfounded by his response, I wondered why. I don't recall his full answer, but I remember the lesson vividly. My father was a compassionate man and was always willing to show up for everyone, even if they didn't show up for him. That is what it means to take the hill. If you show up at your job, but not for the people that count on you, you are a hillfaker.

Taking the hill is about showing up in all aspects of your life and knowing that you are showing up to your highest potential. If you are considering chasing a big goal in your own life, reaching success may feel like an Impossible Hill. I'm here to tell you that nothing is impossible as long as you are willing to show up each day and take one bite out of the elephant at a time.

I know what you are thinking, "Easy for you to say, you've already done it."

That is true, and that's why I am so confident in its truth. I came from nothing, dropped out of college, and started my career on a $16K annual salary. I bootstrapped my life and my business before building an international fitness brand.

If you've ever desired to create your own business, or if you've started your journey as an entrepreneur, and especially if you've created momentum building a company.

You already know how difficult yet very important it is to remain motivated, develop emotional resilience, and lead a team with integrity. In fact, most small businesses fail within the first two years, and 98% of business owners never scale beyond regional success.

This book, Impossible Hill delivers a process that gives you the mindset, tools, and blueprint to discover the unstoppable fire within to destroy your limits and take the hill of your dreams.

Anyone can become a hilltaker, and it starts with a decision. A decision that "I am a hilltaker." For example, let's say you are a meat-eater. You have lived your entire life eating steak but decide overnight that you are now a vegetarian. Yet, that decision will be tested when you eat your next meal. It will be tested again three days from now when your friend asks if you want to come over and grill out steaks. That is the point of the analogy. You become a vegetarian when you decide to become a vegetarian. But, you must solidify that decision over and over with each decision you make.

Coming from the fitness industry, I have seen the recurring patterns where people say they are ready to take the hill with their health, only to burn out and stop coming to the gym a week later. You are a hilltaker just by showing up to the gym. However, it's day 11, when your body is sore, and your motivation fades. That is when your actions solidify the decision of who you are and give your mind the evidence that you indeed are a hilltaker.

This is not a book on theory; there are plenty of those in the market place. These are conclusions based on real-life experiences and over 35 years of success running businesses. This book will explore how to stop killing your progress, how to solidify your decisions, and how to back them up with proof, both physically and mentally. This book will share how you can clarify your vision and your North star—creating momentum, enrolling yourself in your vision while also inspiring the people around you to believe in your vision.

Finally, this book will be a blueprint to help you remove the sandbags in your life and use fear as your superpower. You will learn how to create a manageable cadence in your life that leads to consistent growth and progress instead of burnout. This process is called the hilltaker method, and it helped me bootstrap a company from one location to over 6000+ locations in 28 countries across multiple brands. After you understand the principles laid out in this book, you will be equipped with everything you need to climb the impossible hills in your own life.

Chapter 2

THE UNCERTAIN PATH

We all have big dreams and goals in our lives. There are a few reasons why most people never quite reach them. Many people will start with enthusiasm, only to get discouraged and stop once they meet resistance. Others never take the first step. These are the people you always hear, saying, "One day, I'll start on my dreams." It's not that they are unequipped to chase their dreams. Most people never start because they are afraid. Afraid of failing, afraid of looking bad or uncertain about themselves because the path has not yet been explored. Some people are afraid of success because of the uncertainty that success brings. The majority have found their place of comfort and may never leave it. Fear is a dream killer, and doubt is fear's closest cousin.

However, fear is also normal and can be used as your biggest asset if you will allow it. If your goals are big enough, you should feel a little bit of fear. If you are not afraid, you might want to reevaluate your vision, as your vision may not be big enough. Fears' biggest enemy is progress, and once you get started, and progress follows, you will realize that your fears were mostly in your head.

For example, I have seen thousands of people walk into a health club with big fitness goals. Maybe they want to lose weight, maybe they want to gain weight, or maybe they just want to feel healthier. No matter what the goal is, we all have insecurities because we desire improvement and want better for ourselves. We all share those insecurities. Often, we allow our minds to take over, telling us how difficult that growth will be. It can sound like an impossible hill.

It's easy to imagine ourselves being in great shape, or building a successful business. But it may be difficult to start because we know how much work it will take to achieve our goals. We all struggle with paralysis by analysis sometimes, and if we're not careful, it can stop us from trying. Don't put so much pressure on yourself to achieve your goals right away. Nothing significant was ever accomplished overnight.

One question I ask every person is, "how would you eat an elephant?"

The answer? One bite at a time.

Many people lose momentum because they are busy creating plans, timelines, and roadmaps that likely won't be applicable three months from now. I like to call this "work avoidance" and it all comes back to the fear of starting. People would rather visualize themselves losing weight or starting that business, because it's easier to fantasize about possibility instead of doing the work. Although there is an uncertain path, you can find certainty that you can predict if you push beyond your fears.

Further, what is the outcome if you never start? That answer is staring at you right now and grows every day. It's called regret. Every day I think about the end of my life and the legacy I will leave behind for my children. What lessons do I want to leave with them? How do I want to show up in my life? How do I want them to remember me?

I am grateful for the hard work, the long hours, the tough breaks, and the setbacks. Why? Because it all led me to reach success, and I valued it so much more once I achieved it. On your journey, you will begin to understand that it is the progress and people you encounter along the way that makes success worth chasing. As you will find in this book, there is no such thing as an overnight success. There is only infinite progress on your journey towards success. It all starts with one step in the right direction.

Once you take the first step in the gym and turn on the treadmill for the first time, you start solidifying proof and trust with yourself. You are a hilltaker. I want you to understand your North star at this stage, which I will define as your big goal. What you must do is take the first step because fears' biggest enemy is progress and momentum. Start by walking on the treadmill at 2.5 MPH for one mile. You shouldn't worry about losing 100 pounds at the beginning of your journey. It's the infinite, compounded progress that will eventually lead to climbing your impossible hill. The next day you walk 1.25 miles, the next 1.5, and before you know it, showing up to the gym isn't as scary as it was before. These new habits will get easier each day you do them, and you will continue to solidify your new identity.

At this stage, you might be worried about sprinting or lifting weights, but you've long passed your fear of going to the gym. These are the short-term mindsets and checkpoints that will help you create consistent progress. Progress is motivating, progress is inspiring, and progress breeds confidence. Beyond the growth you see in your body, your mind will grow equally. Every day, just by showing up, your mind begins to believe a little more. Belief is the key ingredient to hit your North star and the discipline to keep showing up will make sure you reach it.

If you are someone that struggles with confidence or getting started, ask yourself how you can trick your mind into believing that it's possible. Maybe you are not confident in your new business yet but think about the part of your life where you are confident. For me, that was racquetball. When I took over my first fitness club, I had fitness experience from playing racquetball but had no management experience. However, I had the confidence to do it because I had spent my entire life succeeding on the racquetball court. Confidence comes through repetition, and I'm willing to bet you have that confidence somewhere in your life right now.

My confidence came from my racquetball experience because of the discipline, accountability, work ethic, and sacrifice it took to succeed. I was committed and had put in so many dedicated hours; it was easy to feel confident on the court. That confidence also led me to quit school altogether and pursue my next venture.

I was a junior at St. Cloud State in Minnesota. Myself and my twin brother were playing racquetball professionally while attending school. One day, I made a decision that would change my life forever. I closed my textbook, looked at my brother, and said, "I quit." My brother looked at me for a moment, then shut his textbook and said, "Well, I quit too." That was how we rolled. We made decisions quickly, even if other people didn't understand it. We had the confidence that we would figure it out, and we were always trying to one-up each other. That competitive nature has served me for my entire life.

We finished out the semester, living in the dorms while still playing racquetball. After the semester, we returned home to Minnesota. We still hadn't told our parents that we quit school, and I still didn't know what I would do with the rest of my life. I took a visit to our local health club to get some practice in, and I could tell the club was failing. It was easy to see that the club was poorly managed and that it wouldn't be around much longer at this pace.

I decided to do something bold. I walked up to the owner and told him that if he ever wanted to turn the club around, he should give me a call. I had no experience running a health club, but I had the confidence that I could figure it out. After all, I had a successful popcorn stand when I was eight, and I had built a successful racquetball career. I knew the work ethic, discipline, and accountability that made me successful in racquetball would also make me successful in whatever I decided to do next.

Maybe it was false confidence at the time, but I had the belief that I could do it. Think back in your life, before people told you that you couldn't. You were probably confident, courageous, and full of enthusiasm. You might not have known what you were doing yet, but you had an unstoppable fire for life. That's where I was in my life, and that's the fire I want to inspire you to rediscover.

Often in our lives, we let our failures put out our unstoppable fire. Maybe it was a coach that told you that you weren't good enough. Maybe a teacher called you stupid. Perhaps it was your parents that taught you to play it safe in life. Somewhere along the way, we are taught to play it safe. We are taught that life is scary, and decisions should be made conservatively. I'm here to tell you that ignorance on fire will beat genius on ice every time.

I was just a kid from Willmar, Minnesota. A racquetball playing dropout with no degree. But you couldn't tell me that I wasn't going to be successful. I may have been ignorant at the time, but my ignorance was on fire, and I didn't care about failing in front of my peers. In fact, I had convinced myself that the club would be successful the moment they called me back.

I didn't hear back from the owner until a year later. The club had finally accepted my offer and presented a proposal to me with a whopping $16,000 a year salary and an incentive to turn the club around. The incentive was a promise. They told me if I could turn the club around, they would let me buy them out with the profits. That may not seem like much, but I had the confidence and belief in myself to turn the club around. I had also been thinking about the opportunity for an entire year and had a plan to make my goal a reality. I said yes and opened a bank account to invest a portion of the profits towards a note at the bank.

At that point, I knew exactly what my goal was. I was going to turn the club around and buy them out. Once I solidified that decision, I wasn't going to let anything stand in my way.

Now I'm going to teach you my process, which has become a foundation in the pillars of my success. I call this 3-step process The Hilltaker Method.

Step 1: Solidify Your Decision

This is where most people begin to stall because they begin to ask all of the "what if" questions. What if I fail? What if I can't do it? Instead, you have to solidify your decision by understanding where you are going. I certainly didn't intend to work at a health club my whole life. I was going to get laser-focused on building that one club and eventually create more clubs all over the country. I wasn't afraid of what people thought. I didn't care if people saw me starting from the bottom. I had nothing to lose and changed the questions I had to positive ones.

Where am I going? Why am I doing this? What if I can turn it around? What if I can be successful?

When people are fearful, they usually turn to three options. Fight, flight, or freeze. You can take the hill and attack that fear through action. You can run away from your fear, or you can fail to make a decision at all. Most people run away from their fear or freeze when opportunities come their way. They listen to their mind, and all of those fears stop them from chasing their dreams.

In the past, you may have lacked the confidence or certainty to chase your dreams, but not anymore. You've made the commitment to keep showing up and take one step at a time towards your North star. A hilltaker shows up and decides, "this is who I am, and this is where I'm going." Once you know your North star and take your first step towards it, you begin to solidify your new identity and build confidence with every step you take.

What is your North Star?

Your North star represents your unwavering purpose. Your mission and deepest desired outcome. Once you know what your North star is, every action moves you closer to that north star or further away from it. It also helps you remove fear from the equation. By understanding that my north star was to buy the club, I wasn't worried about failing. At that point, the club was already failing, and I had college loan debt. I was worried about making sure it was a success. Failure was not an option.

Step 1 starts with solidifying who you are, what your North star is, and taking the first step towards it.

Think of your own North star right now and write it down.

My North star is

_____

_____

_____

_____

Step 2: Clarify Your Vision

Once you have made the decision on your North star and what it is you are striving for, you have to decide what you are willing to sacrifice to achieve your goals. You have to get clear on what needs to be done and enroll yourself in your vision. Your decision will require discipline and starts by setting your own standards for how you want to show up.

On the first day when I walked into the club, my job was to make sure I shared my vision with everyone else at the club. I was 22 years old at the time, but I knew my job was to lead, mentor, and be an example for the employees at the club. The club was failing, but it wasn't the employees' fault. They never had anyone setting the example or pushing them to level up. Nobody expected much from them, and because the bar was set so low, most of the employees had no idea that the club was failing. There was no accountability in the business, starting with leadership. Most of them were showing up for a part-time gig and a paycheck at a health club.

It was up to me to set a new standard, but I knew I couldn't be a dictator, or nobody would follow me. I had to take the lead and hope that people would follow me. I started off with a staff meeting. I let everyone know that the club was failing. I shared exactly why the club was failing and told them the place was a mess. We couldn't show up like this anymore, or we would all be out of a job soon.

I had to set the standard that we were going to run things differently, and the easy fix was to start by cleaning the club. Immediately one of the employees raised her hand and said, "excuse me, we don't clean here." She wasn't condescending; cleaning simply wasn't in their job description at the time.

This was an opportunity to raise the standards on day one. When you are a hilltaker, you will have uncomfortable moments. She simply wasn't aware of how much work and effort it would take to rebuild this failing club. For me, cleaning was a statement that we care about the club, and even though it wasn't in her job description, we were willing to go the extra mile to raise our standards. She wasn't willing to meet those standards, so I had to respond.

"That's fine if you don't clean, but you also don't have a job here anymore," pointing towards the door behind me.

It was a bold statement and not something I enjoy doing, but leadership means making difficult decisions sometimes. I wasn't asking them to do anything that I wasn't willing to do. Remember, leadership is not a dictatorship. Leadership is a willingness to do whatever it takes. I learned those qualities from my father, who would stock shelves and bag groceries if that's what was required.

I insisted, "I'll take the bathrooms." This was an important message because I wanted people to understand that I wasn't above them. Sure, maybe I was in charge, but I was willing to roll up my sleeves and get dirty if it meant our club would be successful. Leadership is about getting people to walk on fire for you, which only happens if you are willing to lead by example. This was a lesson I had learned from my father. I was above nobody in the company, and no task was beneath me.

Remember, my goal was to make sure the club was successful, and I had to make sure everyone knew my vision.

After the meeting finished, I grabbed a mop and started cleaning the bathrooms. We immediately set a new standard for how the club would operate moving forward. My job was to set the standards and hope people would follow. Sure enough, they did, and the club began to turn around.

Once you have clarified your decision, you must decide what you are willing to sacrifice to reach your North star. Let's talk about the word sacrifice because most people view it negatively. Sacrificing is an investment in what you really want—sacrificing what you want now for what you want most. Be willing to sacrifice average to chase great. I was investing every minute into making my dream a reality, and I was committed to reaching my North star.

Every minute was spent in my club or promoting my club. Every day I was solidifying my decision on how the club would look, how it would operate, and how people felt when they walked in the front door. I wanted everyone in town to know where we were and what we were about. I was willing to do whatever it took because failure was not an option.

I still remember the early days of running the club. My commitment was tested, and it was the closest I ever got to giving up. Payroll was due the next day, and I'll never forget the feeling of not having enough money to cover payroll. I was responsible for the employees' livelihood, and if they didn't get paid, I knew how much that would hurt their families. I couldn't let that happen.

I remember breaking down to my mother, telling her that I didn't know what to do. These are the gut check moments where you have to go back to your North star and remember why you are working so hard. I knew I would do anything to make sure I hit payroll. The next morning, a few member prospects came in to sign up for memberships, and they paid their yearly membership in full. It was a blessing I will never forget. Fortunately, I was able to make payroll, and I was never put in that situation again.

Enrolling yourself and your team is only part of achieving your North star. Once you are committed, most people forget to tell the people closest to them. You should also enroll your family and people closest to you. If you are starting a new business and you don't share your vision with your significant other, don't be surprised when they are upset because you are working until 10 pm every night. If you fail to enroll the people around you, they may end up resenting you in the long run.

If you are starting a new business, make sure your family and close friends understand your North star. Let them know what you are doing and why you are doing it. Remember, your job isn't to convince them why you should do it. You have already made the decision that nothing will stop you from reaching your goals. Instead, enroll them by sharing your vision with them and ask for their support. Even if they don't agree with you, clarifying your vision and enrolling your family will make your life a lot easier along your journey towards success.

Step 3: Apply Action

Once you understand your North star and clarify your vision, it's time to apply action towards your North star. Applying action is an infinite progress game that never stops. Sometimes this starts with subtraction. Progress starts when you stop digging deeper holes and remove the sandbags that are holding you back.

To understand the metaphor, let me paint you a picture. You could have a hot air balloon on a perfect day and a full tank of fuel. You pull and pull, lighting a fire underneath the hot air balloon, but it still won't fly. There was nothing wrong with the hot air balloon or the fuel. The problem was that you forgot to untie the sandbags keeping you on the ground.

That is also true in our lives and holds most people back from reaching their goals. For some, the sandbags may represent friends or family members that don't support you. For a business startup, the sandbags could mean canceling Wednesday poker night with your friends or reducing unnecessary spending on the weekends. For some, that might mean trading the snacks in your freezer for the healthy body you want. Are you willing to sacrifice good to achieve greatness?

Once you cut your sandbags, whatever those might be, you are free to pursue your north star with unrelenting focus and infinite progress. You know exactly what you are doing and why you are doing it. You know who supports your vision and remove any obstacles in your path. Now, your sacrifice is part of the progress towards reaching your goals. It becomes less of a sacrifice and more of a time investment towards your North star.

Remember to align your North star with your passion because you will be taking steps towards your North star forever. Your North star isn't a destination; it's a direction. Success doesn't happen overnight, and you will never be able to stop progressing. Make sure you are embarking on a journey worth pursuing.

Make sure your North star lights an unstoppable fire within you that can't be put out, no matter what stands in your way.

This is your opportunity to start over. If you lacked the confidence, discipline, or commitment to quit looking back to the past, consider this your blank canvas. In the past, you didn't have the vision or path to conquer the impossible hills in your life. Now you do, and if at any point in your journey you lose track, come back to these three steps.

1. **Solidify your decision:** Make your decision and get started by taking the first step. Progress will help you solidify your identity that you are a hilltaker, reaffirming your belief that you can accomplish your goals. Progress creates confidence and turns fear into your biggest asset. When you create a belief in your mind by taking action, you are setting yourself up to succeed.

2. **Clarify your vision:** What is your North star? What are you willing to accept from yourself and others? What are you willing to sacrifice? How can you enroll others in your north star so that they support you? Clarify your vision by enrolling yourself first. Establish the direction for achieving your North star. Once you know exactly where you are going, enroll the people in your life that matter the most.

3. **Apply Action:** Start by removing sandbags and obstacles holding back your progress. Once you remove those obstacles, move forward with the idea of infinite progress. When you start creating progress towards your goals,

that progress never stops, which is why it's so important to choose a North star that you are passionate about. To create progress, you must create movement by taking steps forward—one step at a time towards your goal. Progress creates movement, and movement leads to inspiration because you can see yourself getting closer to that vision. Applying action and setting milestones along the way to track your progress will help you remain motivated on the journey to reach the top of your impossible hill.

Most people never stay focused long enough to gain traction toward their goals. Anytime you encounter an impossible hill in your life, it's easy to get overwhelmed. Most people never start because they look at step 10 before they take step 1. Many end up going from idea to idea without ever accomplishing their true North star. Think about your goals long term and decide that you are going to master that industry, no matter how long it may take.

In 5 years, I took the business from losing $200K per year to making $250K per year. It didn't happen overnight, and it took perspective to understand how long it would take to reach my goals. Be patient and give yourself enough time to master your skills and gain traction within each position. That might mean you take a position in the industry of your choice so that you can learn on the job.

If you are passionate about hospitality and eventually want to own a chain of hotels, you might want to start working at the front desk. You will learn how to develop customer service skills and the daily operations of running a hotel. You might not be passionate about the position, but show management that you are willing to sacrifice in the short term for your vision. When you go through the interview process, let them know that your eventual goal is to run your own hotel, and you are willing to do the work to gain that valuable experience. By starting at the bottom and working your way up, you will give yourself the best possible opportunity to be successful when you do own a hotel in the future.

Start by visualizing what you want, create an action plan, set realistic timelines, and goals to keep you moving. Some people spend their entire lives, jumping from one position to another. They look back and realize that they never spent enough time in any position to become great.

If that sounds like you, it's not your fault. Until now, you may not have understood the commitment and sacrifice that is necessary to reach these impossible hills. If you don't believe you can reach your goal, why would you ever start? The hilltaker method starts with the belief that you can accomplish your dreams.

My goal is to inspire you to create an unstoppable fire and reclaim your certainty through small actions each and every day. Taking the hill of your dreams starts with a decision. It begins by saying "I AM A HILL TAKER AND NOTHING WILL STAND IN MY WAY." Find that confidence and passion that once lived inside you and convince yourself that it is truly possible because it is.

You don't have to do it all in one day, one month, or one year. As you will see in future chapters, Snap Fitness was an idea that didn't even begin until I had 20 years of experience running health clubs. It all started with a North star and a solidified decision. I was going to create health clubs all over the United States, and it didn't matter how long it took or what got in my way. I was committed, and I was willing to sacrifice each day to make sure I could eventually reach that goal.

Once I solidified my decision, I took my first step when I took over my first club. I clarified my big vision with myself, the staff, and my family because I knew exactly where I was going. Once everyone in my life was on board, I applied consistent action each and every day. Again, this meant having the discipline to understand where I wanted to go and sacrificing everything else.

On weekends, instead of playing golf or spending time with my friends, I would load up the water coolers and head to the local soccer fields. I spent all day rolling around the cooler, handing out waters and Mr. Freeze pops to the parents at the field. I would pass out waters and 2-week free memberships to our club because I knew I would do whatever it took to drive business into my club.

Everything you hope to accomplish in life will take time. Try to avoid the trap of quitting too soon. Instead, find what you are passionate about and decide that you are going to master it, no matter how long it takes. Clarify where you want to go and commit to sacrificing what you want now, for what you want most. Finally, apply action by taking one step at a time towards your North star and create milestones to keep you motivated. Progress will always give you the perspective on how far you have come on your journey and will keep you inspired to keep moving forward, even when times are difficult. Success is a byproduct of discipline, commitment, and accountability towards your dreams.

Chapter 3

INFINITE PROGRESS

Starting a business, you are passionate about is so essential because the progress never ends. Some people assume that once your business is successful, you can sit back and count your money. Most don't realize that while getting started is the key, the progress never ends. Once famously, Steve Jobs said that if you wanted to go into business for yourself, you had to be a little crazy. Why would you ever want to work so hard for so long and still have a 90%+ chance of failure? Many businesses fail because they didn't set the right expectations, and they weren't passionate about what they were doing. Even Steve Jobs, who became one of the most iconic innovators of our lifetime, didn't get to fully see his vision to the end before he passed. Apple was over 40 years in the making and still continues to innovate towards its original North star.

It is easy to chase the idea of money. Everyone wants to make money, but that chase is elusive. Money is too fast to chase, and if you chase it, you will find yourself burnt out and exhausted because you started for the wrong reasons. Instead, start with your passion because you will be committed to chasing down your dream for the rest of your life. That is the idea of infinite progress.

In the health space, I wasn't thinking about multi-million dollar exits. Instead, I became obsessed with improving our process for our members. Every day I was studying the latest trends, ideas, and trade publications, to make sure I was educated on what our members wanted now and in the future. My job was to make sure my product was always relevant and consistent with my customers' expectations. I was providing the best product for our customers as times as the industry evolved.

Infinite progress is about understanding the long road ahead and setting the right expectations to navigate that road. Even after Snap Fitness reached more than 1000 locations, we still hadn't officially made it. Companies like Blockbuster, who had over 9,000 locations, and Dominos with over 17,000, both learned quickly that business never stops. One company rested on their success and they no longer exist. The other admitted they were failing and made drastic changes to fix it.

As the industry and consumer behavior changed, we needed to evolve as well. Once we hit 1000 locations, we had to pivot and set the market again. We added heart rate-based training, added group fitness, functional training, and created fitness challenges throughout the year. The industry and customers' expectations changed. The consumer was becoming much more knowledgeable about exercise and what it takes to get fit. We had to evolve and adapt accordingly to deliver on our customer experience.

You must be on fire and fall in love with your business, otherwise, someone with more fire will come along and put you out of business. It's a painful lesson that most people learn the hard way because they were in it for the wrong reasons.

Before you start that next idea, ask yourself if you would do that every day for the rest of your life, even if you didn't get paid. Don't get me wrong; money is significant. You can help a lot more people with money than you can without it. But you must be prepared to work day in and day out towards your North star, or you will end up like Blockbuster.

Blockbuster thought that success would last forever. At its peak in the late 90's, Blockbuster owned over 9,000 video-rental stores in the United States, employed 84,000 people worldwide, and had 65 million registered customers. Blockbuster was valued as a $3 billion company and earned as much as $800 million on late fees alone.

The owner of Blockbuster became complacent in their market place and thought it was an everlasting profit machine. Instead of focusing on embracing technology and staying relevant to consumers' expectations, they were slow to react to the competitive landscape. Very quickly, their product became obsolete. Blockbuster was focused on what worked for them in the past instead of looking towards the digital future of streaming.

This is why vision is such an important component of success. Blockbuster should have seen what the future had in store and acquired Netflix for 50 million when they had the opportunity. Instead, they let their ego get in the way, and eventually, Blockbuster was gone. I remember to this day, buying Blockbuster locations for Snap Fitness, swearing I would never let this happen to me.

Dominos pizza was facing the same destiny if they didn't make drastic changes. Dominos built a pizza empire and a world recognized brand, but they also built a reputation during the early 2000's as the worst pizza chain (by real consumer reports). Instead of brushing that reputation under the rug, they had to reinvent themselves. They could have done what their competitors did and said they had improved their ingredients, but instead, they took the hilltaker method to heart.

Dominos started by acknowledging that their pizza quality no longer met their expectations. They even ran commercials telling customers they knew their pizza was terrible, and they were committed to upgrading it. They started a wave of transparency in their marketing and even showed the public how they took pictures to make the pizza look better. Beyond that, Dominos fans had no reason to be excited about the product. They just liked the fast, affordable pizza.

Dominos took massive action to change their business. They changed their ingredients, their messaging, and remodeled their stores. At one point, they even decided to start filling potholes to make sure their customers' pizzas arrived in tact. Dominos began to focus on solving problems, not growing profits.

Domino's Pizza is now acclaimed as one of the best rebrands over the last ten years. From 2009 to 2016, they went from a 9% to 15% share in the pizza restaurant market. They knew that competitors were coming for them, and they had to make drastic changes to survive. At the beginning of 2020, the results speak for themselves. They have over 17,000 retail locations in 90 countries and estimated global retail sales to be $14.3 billion in 2019.

The concept of infinite progress doesn't mean that you don't take time to appreciate how far you've come. In fact, it's necessary to celebrate those milestones along the way. Take a moment and appreciate your accomplishments and all of the people you have helped. Be careful not to let that appreciation turn into complacency. Once you climb to the top of one mountain, start looking for your next mountain to climb.

It's also critical that you share the success of the company with your people. Once per quarter, I would share the progress of our company, give accolades to top performers, set new goals, and ask where we can get better. It's essential to recognize your success to keep yourself, and your team inspired, but always set new goals aimed towards your North star. A leader can bring vision, ambition, passion, and motivation, but you can't achieve your vision by yourself. When your team does a great job, make sure to celebrate those milestones and start climbing your next mountain. The journey and progress never ends.

Even with great people around you, it will require consistent, concentrated focus, one step, and one day at a time. If you wanted to boil a pot of water, that pot must reach and sustain 212 degrees. If you leave the pot on the fire, it boils. You can't turn the stove on and off. This is why it's so important not to spread yourself thin or dilute your attention as you go. This is why leadership is so vital for the continued success of your business.

In order to grow, you have to be willing to lead with action and get people to walk on fire for you. The book, The E-Myth shares the key to why most small businesses fail. Most people think that because they are good at the skill they perform at their job, they are automatically qualified to run a business. The fatal assumption that an individual who understands the technical work of a business can successfully run a business that does that technical work. Your job is to set clear expectations, discipline based on your North star, hold people accountable to those expectations, and be able to measure your progress. Remember, progress never ends.

If you are doing every task in your business, or if your business solely relies on you, then you don't have a business; you have a job. It will also be challenging, if not impossible, to sell your business to a successor, especially if it requires you to be in it to operate.

Here are the four steps to creating a process and bringing others with you:

1. **Setting expectations/Creating process:** Some people think they should be applauded just for showing up. I set the expectation right away that although I am the CEO, I will shovel the walk, I will clean the bathrooms, and I am above no person and no task. That level of gratitude sets the expectation for everyone else in the organization. Your job is to bring everyone else with you, not to tell them where to go. The core values of your company must be indoctrinated into every person, starting with you. I was creating a culture that supports a good work ethic, personal accountability, and good teamwork. Additionally, creating standardized processes and procedures with input from your organization will help with that teamwork and understanding of each person's responsibilities. How you show up will create a trickle-down effect throughout your entire organization.

2. **North star navigation:** Once you know your North star, your job is to uphold your expectations while focusing on every decision to move you closer to your North star. Your ability to grow your company will depend on how well you transfer your skillsets to your team and how well you discipline the standard you set for yourself and your company. Remember, your people will only show up based on the standards to uphold in your company. It starts with how you show up both personally and professionally. If you

teach people what you know, and they know that you care about them, they will walk on fire for you.

3. **Accountability to a higher standard:** When you bring someone into your organization, make sure they are upholding the core values that you set. In future chapters, we will discuss the levels of discipline. If you set your standards high and indoctrinate those standards within the culture of your company, people will uphold them. If they don't, it's up to you to hold them accountable. If you do this the right way while building your culture, you won't ever have to fire someone. They will either raise their own standards, or they will opt out and find somewhere else to work. Remember, don't pull people up; bring them with you.

4. **Tracking & Measuring:** What you track, you can measure. In the early stages of your business, you must track where every dollar is being spent and how your business is growing. It's nearly impossible to scale your business without a complete understanding of costs vs. revenue. If your business is growing, understand why and if that growth is sustainable. If your business isn't growing, find out what is keeping the company stagnant. Are their outside factors affecting your growth? Competitors? An event that shifted the market place? I knew exactly what all of my competitors were doing. I knew how many flyers I needed to hand out to bring in a new member prospect and knew what my operating expenses were in granular detail. Don't allow yourself to become reactive in your business. Be accountable

to your numbers, so you know exactly what is growing your bottom line and where you are wasting valuable resources.

It took me over eight years to make good on my promise of buying that first health club. It took one day at a time, knowing that my North star was to one day own their facility and, God willing, expand it to multiple locations. I knew that small decisions each day would compound into reaching my goals. Every extra penny I made, I invested in purchasing the club. Most people spend a few weeks or months working on a dream before deciding it's not worth it. That is the myth of entrepreneurship. Real success takes concentrated, compounded effort for years at a time. In the next chapter, we will talk about those hill fakers that have sold you a lie.

Eight years might sound like a long time, but it set me up for future success. I wasn't over-leveraged with debt, and after I sold my first club, I was looking for my next hill to climb. I leveraged my first club with a bank to secure a loan to build a second club. After paying off the second club, I repeated the process on the third club. Twenty years after saying yes to the opportunity to turn around my first club, I had seven clubs total before selling them all. After 20 years of hard work, commitment, and sacrifice, I had $3 million to my name. My journey was only beginning.

That's what Infinite progress is all about. Your journey never stops. You just set your North star towards a bigger impossible hill and start climbing. One step at a time, one foot in front of the other. At this point, I was left wondering what I would do next. I wasn't a kid anymore. I had a wife, along with three young children. Still, there was another hill to climb.

A former employee came to me and shared that he didn't like whom I sold the clubs to. He asked me if I would build a different concept for him. Instead of a full traditional health club, what if we created a concept that had everything someone would need to get fit while removing the extras. We took out the swimming pools, childcare, racquetball courts, and aerobics classes. We reduced the size of the club from 40,000 sq feet to 4,000, and instead of appealing to 100% of people, we were now appealing to 70%. Sure, there were people that wouldn't come because we didn't have the extra amenities, but the smaller club allowed us to be nimble and convenient.

We built the first club in an urban market, and in 90 days, it was cash-flow positive. I built a second one in a mid-level market and, again, cash flow positive in 90 days. Finally, I decided to build one in a small town to see if this success would duplicate. It was a success, and at that moment I knew I had a tiger by the tail.

This was the opportunity of a lifetime, and I had to go for it. The entire time I'm solidifying my decision and creating self-evidence because it was working. Every location we built was successful, and my confidence grew that a franchise model would be possible.

In future chapters, we will discuss the myth of scale. I could have raised money to open those clubs or brought on investors, but

I didn't need to. I was in complete control of the direction of the company, and now I had market validation. The dogs were eating the dog food. Every location we built, no matter the market, was cash flowing within the first 90 days. I could have gone to investors or banks to raise capital. The longer you can go without taking outside money, the more control you have to build your company. I knew we had something big that could be franchised all over the world, but we had to move quickly.

Remember the hilltaker method, one of the most important parts is enrolling the people in your life. I was 100% committed to my North star, and I had to make sure my wife and three kids knew where we were going. I had just spent the last 20 years working to build a great life. I just sold my company, and I was going right back into battle. They needed to know why I was starting Snap Fitness and that we would all have to make sacrifices to set our family up forever.

I sat down with my wife and children, who were 1, 3, and 5 at the time. They had watched how hard I was working, and I shared my vision with them. I asked them for a 5-year window to go all-in for our family. Not just for our family, but for the next generations to come. I shared that it would require hard work, discipline, and sacrifice not only from me, but from them as well. There would be days I would need to work long hours and times I would have to travel as we were building.

This was my moment, similar to when my father sat us down and said we were moving to Willmar, Minnesota. I was setting the table for my family that I was going into battle, and failure was not an option. With my family in support, I set off to build my empire.

My decision was already solidified, and I had full confidence that Snap Fitness would be successful. It was already working, and we were gaining momentum. The momentum wasn't going to stop as long as we kept pushing forward. Once my vision was clear, and my family supported me, we were full steam ahead. Our obstacles at this time were the racquetball courts, swimming pools, aerobic studios, and childcare. We removed all of the overhead and set ourselves up to scale with speed.

Our process was refined. Every employee and franchisee knew what our North star was. Every one of our clubs was opened with a punch list of items. I knew, in chronological order, the exact process to open each store. From the real estate to customer retention, I knew where each location was and what stage it was at. Understanding every detail allowed us to scale at speed with very few setbacks. Many companies scale too quickly and fail because they forget to solidify a simple, can't fail process. We ensured that any franchisee would be successful as long as they went through our process and worked hard.

Even as Snap Fitness scaled nationally to over 1000 locations, I knew that we would have to pivot with the market. Infinite progress never ends. Markets shift, technology evolves, and consumers want change constantly. I knew as our model continued to gain momentum, there would be competitors coming to market to share in our success. Initially, it was enough to lean on our core differences.

1. Snap Fitness was open 24-hours

2. No contract, no obligation: we had to earn your business and your trust every day.

3. State of the art equipment

4. Reciprocity: If you're a member at one club, you have access to all clubs worldwide.

Ten years later, we had to grow our footprint to be more accessible. We saw the success of boutique functional training studios, discount players, and numerous brands that focused on group fitness. We didn't want to become the next Blockbuster. We focused on adding group fitness classes and functional training because that's what the market was telling us. We noticed that heart rate training was becoming more popular, so we introduced heart monitors so our members could stay accountable to their workout goals. We increased our staffed hours. We educated our staff on nutrition, diet, and effort to help articulate what's necessary to reach your wellness goals.

That's what the market told us they wanted, and it forced us to pivot to meet that demand. This is why this chapter is called infinite progress and why it's so important to find a category you are passionate about. The progress never ends, and neither will the competition. There will always be someone trying to take what you have built.

If you are entering new territory and you are successful, be prepared to constantly innovate because your competitors will be coming after your marketplace advantage. You should always be adjusting your vision and goal every time you reach it. The greatest companies do that, while many sit and rest on their success. It's up to you to focus your attention and efforts on infinite progress as you continue to evolve your product offering and your brand.

Chapter 4

HILLFAKERS

"Comparanoia" has created an easy trap for aspiring entrepreneurs to step in. Some people might call it keeping up with the Joneses. There is more pressure than ever to portray a false sense of reality about your success or financial status, even if you haven't arrived yet. You see people posting pictures of cars they can't afford and buying clothes or fancy dinners to impress people in their lives. If you are over-leveraged, trying to portray a false reality, you may be a hillfaker.

You are not alone; I have been there before myself. I'll never forget in my early days of business. I wanted to buy this Corvette. I had always wanted a Corvette, and my brother, who had already built his first successful business, had just purchased his own. He could comfortably afford it. I didn't want to feel like I was falling behind, so I decided to go for it. The $680 per month payment wasn't more than I could afford at the time, but it was more than I should have been paying. It was outside of my practical needs.

I never missed a payment on that car, but it held back the early progress of my business because I was trying to keep up with my brother. Buying that Corvette slowed down the progress of building my business because I was spending that money on a car instead of investing it into my growth. I had to take a hard look in the mirror and compare wants vs. needs. To this day, every few months, I do a full financial analysis to make sure I am not frivolously spending on things I no longer use or need. It's not that I can't afford it, it's about holding myself accountable regardless of my financial status. All of the small things add up, and it can become death by 1000 cuts for your financial future if you're not aware.

It's easy to fall into the same trap I did, and even easier to do it today with everyone sharing their highlight reels on Instagram. Social media has created an inflated reality about success and living the "good life." In reality, we are all flawed, and progress starts by loving that part of yourself. Instead of feeling like you have to fake your reality, learn to love your reality, and embrace the climb of wanting a better life.

85% of small businesses fail, and it's not because they didn't have a great idea. Most of them fail because they were over-leveraged, over digitized, over hyped and they didn't have a clear vision of their North star. They created some success and celebrated or purchased luxuries they didn't need instead of investing back into their business. In the early stages, reinvest everything you can back into your business and build cash reserves in the event you need to pivot in a competitive marketplace. When you invest back into your business, those dollars begin to compound your growth.

It is not worth hurting your future to buy things you don't need, just to impress people. Don't let yourself get overleveraged or behind on your taxes just because you want to buy a fancy watch. There is a reason Mark Zuckerberg wears the same shirt every day. He is focused on his mission, not his appearance. Reinvest that money back into your business early, and you will be able to buy ten of those watches in the future. Be willing to trade good for great.

Take a moment and be honest with yourself right now.

Are you a hillfaker?

If you said yes, I commend you. It is honorable and takes courage to admit that you are faking it, intentionally or unintentionally. The only way to change your situation is to be truthful with your current situation. Your current situation is not your end destination, and if you feel some guilt at this point, use it as fuel to start the hilltaker method from phase 1.

Take ownership of what is making you a fraud. Are you showing up in your business? Your relationships? Your health? Wherever it is, draw a line in the sand and say, "I'm finished avoiding my problems." Many entrepreneurs think that if they make a lot of money, it will fix their relationship. That couldn't be further from the truth.

Please acknowledge that we all make mistakes and that we are all flawed. Once you enter a place of vivid truth, you can take one step at a time in the right direction to change your situation. Life is not about Lamborghinis or social media highlight reels. Keep your focus on your North star vision and take one step at a time. I promise you that while you are focusing on infinite progress, one step at a time, the hillfakers will be treading water in the same place they are now, getting no further than when they started.

Worry less about your image and ego and worry more about the impact and value you want to create in the world. This is your opportunity to create discipline and patience for your future. Do you want to buy a fancy dinner and a nice watch? Or would you rather provide for your kids or support a worthwhile charity that solves global problems? Don't let your ego negatively impact your future by focusing on self-serving ideals. Here is how to realign with what is truly important in your life.

1. **Go back to your North Star:** What do you really want out of life? Who do you want to become? Who is important in your life? What do you value most? Where are you coming up short?

2. **Assess your situation:** Where are you spending your time and money? Track exactly where you are in alignment with your values and acknowledge the truth about your situation. How do you want to show up in life?

3. **Solidify your decision:** Change only happens when the pain of staying the same is greater than the pain of change. Solidify your decision by making progress. Set up an automated savings account, buy groceries instead of eating out, or take that first step on the treadmill. Make a decision and solidify that decision that you are a hilltaker.

4. **Clarify your vision:** Patience and discipline is key. If you've got yourself in debt, you are overweight, or you're living an unhealthy lifestyle, those habits didn't develop overnight. You can't expect to change your situation in a day, a week, or even one year. Take consistent daily action towards your new North star and continue to enroll yourself. You will be tested every day with each decision you make.

5. **Understand your why:** Part of enrolling the people around you, also includes knowing why you are doing what you are doing. Most people start a business because they want freedom to spend more time with their family. However, many eventually end up neglecting their family in the process of pursuing that North star. Understand exactly why you are working towards your goal and keep that in mind when times start to get hard or going through necessary growing pains.

6. **Remove sandbags/apply action:** Again, take consistent action and remove obstacles. If comparing yourself to people on Instagram makes you feel unworthy, delete Instagram, or set more boundaries. If your cabinet is full of cookies and it's

ruining your diet, throw away the cookies. You send a signal to yourself when you make a bold stance towards whom you want to be. Once you know what got you in this situation, you can take steps towards improving the situation and creating the best version of yourself.

Someone once asked me, "Peter, do you want to know how to become the man of your dreams?" Eager for the answer, I said, of course. He simply replied, "all you have to do to become the man of your dreams is to start making every decision like you are already him."

It might be challenging to see yourself as the CEO of a national or multinational company or the physically fit, healthy version of yourself. When you wake up in the morning, decide to start making decisions like you are already that person. Would the CEO of a large company sleep in until 11 AM, or would you be up at 6 AM attacking the day? Would the fit version of yourself skip the gym today, or would your best self-commit to a planned time to exercise, regardless of how early or tired you might be?

This is a practice of discipline and accountability. Can you create the disciplines that will allow you to build the company and life of your dreams? There will be days that you don't feel like showing up. Your accountability will push you to show up even on those difficult days. If you tell yourself, "one day is fine," it can quickly compound in other areas of your life. If you have big dreams and aspirations, hold yourself more accountable for achieving those dreams. Your success will happen because of a series of small decisions, repeated each day. Those repeated events either continue your growth or become detrimental to your vision. Small choices add up to the sum of your life.

Chapter 5

RUDY SYNDROME

Some of you may remember the 1993 film of the storied Rudy. It's a story about a young man who dreams of playing football at Notre Dame. However, he lacked the grades, money, talent, and physical stature to reach that goal.

Still, nothing would deter Rudy from chasing his dream. After two years at Holy Cross and three rejections from Notre Dame, Rudy is finally admitted and attends football tryouts in an attempt to make the team as a "walk-on" player. The coach notices his tenacity, and eventually, Rudy makes the practice squad.

The underdog story ends with Notre Dame leading 17–3. The coach sends all the seniors into the game except Rudy, despite the assistant coaches' urging. Fans, who are aware of Rudy's goal from a story in the student newspaper, start a "Rudy!" chant in the stadium. After much built-up energy in the stadium, the coach finally lets Rudy play on the Notre Dame kickoff to Georgia Tech.

Rudy stays in for the final play, sacks the Georgia Tech quarterback, and is carried around on his teammates' shoulders to cheers from the stadium. It's an all-time underdog story as Rudy defeats the odds to accomplish his dreams of playing Notre Dame football.

Rudy's story has inspired multiple generations never to give up and chase your dreams, no matter who tells you you're crazy. The story of Rudy is an inspiring story of setting goals and chasing those goals until you hit them. Despite all odds, Rudy wasn't willing to quit until he made it on the field. He pursued his dreams with forward progress until he was carried off that field on the shoulders of his teammates.

I love the symbolism of the Rudy story because it shows the value of hustle, perseverance, and effort. However, while Rudy only got to play in the game, he never won a Super Bowl. Once you hit your goals, make sure to appreciate your progress before looking for your next impossible hill to climb.

If you've ever picked up this book, you probably have aspirations to build something great and take the hill of your dreams. For Rudy, playing for Notre Dame was his impossible hill. For you, there are lessons to be learned from Rudy. Yes, you should work hard, persevere, and give great effort. However, you should also set bigger goals and force yourself to level up to reach those bigger goals.

Let me tell you another story that may sound familiar.

In the year 2000, the New England Patriots selected a quarterback with the 199th pick. He was not viewed as much of a prospect. He was slow, awkward, and didn't have great arm strength. None of his physical attributes would lead you to believe he would become an all-time great football player.

That player was Tom Brady, and many now regard him as the greatest quarterback to ever play the game. I am hardly suggesting that Rudy and Tom Brady had similar stories because Tom Brady had far more talent coming into the league. I am suggesting that Tom Brady took his opportunity and became so good they couldn't take him out of the game. Today, he has more than 220 wins, 6 Super Bowls, 14 Pro Bowls, and a list of records that read more like a rap sheet.

However, Tom Brady didn't come into the league a superstar. If you remember his early career, he was more of a game manager, sitting behind the mastery of a great defense and Bill Belichick. In his first six seasons as the team's starter, Brady had established a consistent baseline of success: about 300 completions at a 60 percent rate and around 25 touchdowns. A little less than one interception a game. An adjusted yards-per-attempt rate of 6 or 7. And a lot of wins: 10, 12, even 14 each season.

Brady was focused on betterment every moment of his career. He was focused on refining every one of his physical skills, but he knew that's where his limitations might hold him back. He was never going to have the biggest arm or quickest feet. Instead of accepting his limitations, he maximized his physical potential while focusing on what he could control, his mind.

Brady approached every day with a chip on his shoulder. He remembered the frustration of being picked in the 6th round. He used his critics as fuel and became one of the hardest working, competitive players to ever play the game. He maximized his mental performance, his sleep, his diet and every part of his life that he could control.

Tom Brady would routinely say "good afternoon" to his teammates that arrived at the facility at 6:30 a.m. because he had been there since 5. Brady used everything he could as fuel. His critics became his biggest allies, and his own fears pushed him to make sure they would never become a reality. Brady used every psychological and physical edge he could to become the greatest quarterback of all time.

That is the difference between Tom Brady and Rudy. Sure, Tom Brady could have been content after winning his first Super Bowl. They carried him off the field, and that could have been his Rudy moment. He could have celebrated for a lifetime after winning that Super Bowl. Many of the greatest athletes ever never reached that milestone. But Tom Brady didn't want to be carried off the field and celebrated for one accomplishment. He wanted to be the greatest of all time. This was his North star, driven with much direction and purpose.

Who do you want to emulate? Do you want to get on the field? Or do you want to chase Super Bowls? Do you want to celebrate good or chase great?

There was a point in my life that I thought selling my first health club was my Super Bowl. I thought I had arrived, but that was really just my step from college to the NFL. If I wanted to win Super Bowls and go for great, I had to go all-in and refine my focus even more. I became a man on a mission, and much like Tom Brady, I used everything as fuel. I used my inner critic and outer critics as motivation to keep growing.

My North star was my Super Bowl. My dream was to open fitness clubs across the United States, and I couldn't do that if I was busy celebrating past success. I definitely couldn't do that if I didn't refine our process to create championship results. Every decision was methodical and most importantly, scalable. Focus on results, not the fans in the stands.

I was laser-focused on my goals, and I knew that the Snap Fitness model was the best way to get there. I realized that although Snap Fitness didn't have all of the amenities some larger facilities had, we had everything that somebody needed to get fit.

I took the time to understand the marketplace and evaluate the competition. After realizing that 30% of the exercising public wanted a full-service facility, I made the bet that 70% of the exercising population would love my product and appreciate the value for the price. Given my facilities' size, I could strategically position them in neighborhood strip malls, making them convenient for my members.

I made the bet that most people felt like they were paying for amenities they weren't using, and I went all-in on that bet. Snap Fitness was 1/10th the cost of my earlier full-service gyms, instead of having 50 employees, there were 2. There was less overhead, and our return on capital was 5X that of a full-service gym. My Snap Fitness battle cry in 2004 was "we're a 24-hour, affordable alternative to the typical big gym membership. Our facilities were full of state-of-the-art equipment, no contract, and we have everything you need to reach your fitness goals."

At the end of 2004, on the back of that message, we began franchising. The first year we opened 12 locations. The second-year we opened 60. 3rd year, 180. In the fourth year, we opened more than 250 locations, and by year 5, I had accomplished my goal of opening one location per day. We opened 377 locations in one year before eventually breaking 1000 locations. All of that happened because we simplified our model, reinvested into our business, and compounded our growth.

My original health club success felt like Rudy; it was a victorious venture. However, Snap Fitness was more like Tom Brady. We had that fire and desire to stop at nothing and place no limitations on what was possible. When you refine your focus and set new goals, you can win Super Bowls instead of just getting on the field.

Chapter 6

FUNNEL DREAMS

The word discipline is used a lot in the world of fitness and business. What do you think of when you think of discipline? Most people think negatively. They remember their father saying they were going to discipline them when they got home. People also assume discipline means sacrificing something, aka "I'm going to have the discipline to get up every day at 6 am."

While those are forms of discipline, I think of discipline differently. There are three types of discipline, and they all serve as guidelines, expectations and boundaries that keep our lives or businesses on track towards our North star.

There is a myth that people hold dearly; they say, "If I can just have X happen, I'll lose weight" or "If I could just build a funnel, I'll have an automated million-dollar business." The truth about success in any part of your life is that it's never just one big event. It's a series of disciplines and accountability compounded day after day, year after year, that makes someone successful. Sure, might you get lucky and land a big break? Of course. But that only comes after years and years of compounded discipline that led to your opportunity to receive that big break. Don't assume there is a magic formula for reaching your dreams. There is no magic pill, no transformational diet, and no funnel that will do the work for you. It's up to you and the discipline you set up in your life.

Preventative Discipline

If people don't know the rules, you can't keep score. Imagine a football game without rules. There would be a ball, 22 players, end zones and goal posts, but without rules there would be a lot of running around and chaos. If you don't create the rules of your life and your business, you can expect the same chaos. Many of you might be imagining that image in your head thinking, that would never happen to me. But what rules have you set for yourself? What are your non-negotiables?

Many people start a business, but they forget to set guidelines, expectations, and rules for the game they are playing. Sure, you might be able to reach some success without rules. But anybody can be successful if you set the bar at your ankles. We are aiming for scalable, predictable, and compounded success for the rest of your life.

Set up the rules in your own life and your business, then commit to being accountable to those rules no matter what happens. Part of sacrificing what you want now for what you want most means making a healthier decision or not buying everything you think you want.

For example, you might want to set a goal to save $250 per week, and you are willing to sacrifice to make that a reality. Maybe you cook dinner instead of eating out and decide to make your own coffee. At the end of the week, it's your discipline that says, "I won't compromise on that goal, and I'll figure it out." If you only saved $200 that week, look at where you can cut frivolous spending or increase your income. No matter what it takes, commit to the rules you have set up.

On day one, I walked into my first health club, and I set the expectations and our rules for the club. At the very minimum, I knew that we were going to provide a clean club for our members. Our members were going to feel appreciated and loved every time they walk in the door. We were going to be committed to understanding everyone's wellness goals, and we would hold them accountable to reach their goals. Each day I followed these expectations that I had for myself and every member of our staff.

Everyone had a checklist, and our core values were written on the walls. This is where we decided to set our bar, and we weren't willing to accept anything less. You get what you accept, not what you expect.

Here is a checklist of questions to help you set your own rules for your life and business:

1. What am I passionate about?

2. How do I maintain a positive attitude each day?

3. What are my core values? how do I want to live my life?

4. How will I help others win?

5. How do I want to show up each day regardless of my job or the circumstances I'm in?

6. What are my non-negotiables surrounding my character & brand performance?

7. Objectively what do I want to accomplish today? Set up each day with goals & checklists.

When I run my businesses, some days I'm a firefighter, and others I'm a cruise director. But either way, I know exactly where my ship is heading. That's part of life, and no two days are the same. Make sure you own that no matter what your day holds, you have a set of non-negotiables. Be passionate about your standards and never apologize for holding people to those high standards. Remember, it's your job as a leader to lift others up and let them know that this is a group effort; we win and lose together.

Supportive Discipline

Once you set the rules, you now become the referee. Remember, you should only hold others to the same standards that you set for yourself. This isn't a requirement, but this is a book on leadership, not dictatorship. If I expected the staff to take an interest and show appreciation for our members, I knew I had to be leading from the front. Every morning I had to be greeting customers and showing that same level of appreciation for the staff at our club. I knew that attitude would trickle down through everyone in the organization.

If someone from our staff was wavering from our standards and not treating our members with kindness, it was up to me to course-correct and make sure they knew that behavior was not ok. It made the conversation easy to have because it was indoctrinated on our walls. "Remember, we all agreed that this is how we are going to show up and how we treat our members." It's the job of leadership to lift others up and hold them to a higher standard than they hold themselves.

Supportive discipline doesn't just mean enforcing the rules. Supportive discipline is also how I describe mentorship. Michael Jordan was a great basketball player when he got to the NBA, but he was also very stubborn. He wanted to take every shot, make every play, and put the weight of the world on his back. It took a great coach like Phil Jackson to help him level up and understand he needed to invest in his teammates if he ever wanted to win championships.

Mentorship is a part of leadership, and it requires supportive discipline. Great leaders mentor people and help them level up. Leadership is not titled, and anyone can be a leader, no matter how long they have held a position. Leadership is about taking action and helping others around you. Leadership is about accountability to maintain high standards for yourself and others.

For example, it would be easy for an employee to say, "I'm going to leave early today. I'll follow up on those leads tomorrow." When an employee starts trending in this direction, it's easy to let that behavior slide. However, if you allow it once, they will assume it's ok to do it all of the time. Eventually, they have leads backed up in their inbox, and the membership numbers begin to decline. It can be a pattern that compounds if you don't hold yourself and your staff accountable.

In almost every situation, people will uphold the expectations you set except for a few reasons:

1. **Lack of respect**: If your key players don't trust you and respect you as a leader, they won't follow you. Trust begins with how people feel towards you as a person. How do you show up at the office, in your community, and at home? If the people around you don't respect you, it's usually because they don't trust your vision or trust your ability to lead during tough times. Remember, trust and respect are earned, not given.

2. **Hold everyone equally accountable:** As a leader, make sure you hold everyone to the same standards. Leaders often fall into the trap of playing favorites in their organization. Ensure that you hold your executives and managers to the same standards as your staff and don't give preferential treatment. If you hold people within your organization to a different level of accountability for the same job, you're going to have problems.

3. **Lack of opportunity:** in many cases, people lose respect and passion for what they do if they feel like there's no room for growth or opportunity within the company. Some employees want a paycheck, but most want to feel growth and opportunity. People want to know where they fit into the company's future, and they want to feel valued. Make sure you are providing enough opportunity, so they feel like they are growing and evolving with the company.

4. **Ownership within projects:** it's important you allow people to own specific projects. If you always hover over your team's responsibility or directive, they will feel like you don't respect their ability as a leader. If your leadership doesn't trust you, it's hard to have confidence in a position long term. Empower your people and have confidence in your ability to communicate what it is that you want them to accomplish. Then step back and trust that they can get the job done. If they fail to follow directions, ask yourself how you can better communicate your vision next time?

Corrective Discipline

Anytime you start a new venture, you should always plan for the worst and hope for the best. In most cases, when a project veers off course, it's because the vision was not laid out or articulated in a manner in which people understood it. People can't follow what they can't see. It is the leadership's responsibility to make sure the message is clear and concise. From that point, monitor all material projects closely and pivot accordingly when there is a change in the marketplace.

Share your vision, set forth your plan, and make sure people understand the direction the ship is heading. Once they understand that, they can buy into your vision and execute. Sure, there may be times when the initiative or the key player on your team veer off course, and it's your job to steer back towards your North star. Don't assume that your team has veered off track because they are not listening. Instead, have a conversation, bring them back to their goals, and get back on track. Often, leadership assumes that it is the employees' fault when it's usually just a miscommunication on the task or direction.

Corrective discipline starts with accountability. If you follow the process until this point, you have set your expectations and can course-correct when you get off track. Once you know they understand the expectations, they are competent in their role, and they still are not upholding those expectations, it may be time to have a conversation.

If a project or employee continually needs course-correcting, first try to understand whether the issue is comprehensive or compliance-related. If it's a comprehension issue, take the time to go through the vision again, as these are learning opportunities. You don't want your employees to walk on eggshells, so make sure to articulate your point differently.

If the issue is compliance-related, then that means the employee likely doesn't share in the vision you have set forth. Make sure you listen to their input, so they feel understood. They may have a valid point, but they might not understand the business's full picture. Let them know that you appreciate their input and find a way to return to the company's overall vision if they are still on board and point right back to your North star.

Remember, there are always more diplomatic ways of handling things in your business. If someone requires discipline in my company, under my leadership, I'm asking them, "where does the problem reside?" Is it a conflict between two people? Is it a personality conflict? You've got to identify the conflict. They will likely give you some response that will connect the dots. If it's something serious going on in their life, be compassionate and supportive, but let them know that their effort isn't meeting the companies expectations.

If I am continually having a problem with an individual following direction or the vision, the first question I ask myself is, have I cast the person in the wrong role with-in my company?

Then follow up by asking, is there a position that's better suited for them?

If the person in question has a negative effect on the people around them, then we have an issue that's greater than repositioning them. If someone has a toxic personality, it's important to address it right away to avoid spreading toxicity through our entire division or company. Once again, the first question I ask myself is this a comprehension problem or compliance. Both should be treated very differently.

Over my 35-year career, you would be surprised; the right people will come back the next day and say thank you for not giving up on them. Instead of giving up on people and firing fast, first, try to help them level up. Remember, your job as a leader is to mentor your people. Firing someone is the easy way out, but it also means you have to replace their work. If you can help people realize that their effort or attitude is detrimental to the vision and goals of the company, it allows them the opportunity to reflect and grow.

They will come back with a fire in their belly, ready to go to work. You also save yourself the headache as you scale because you took steps one and two, setting the expectations. If they continually fail to meet expectations after multiple conversations, then they are opting out once you have the difficult conversation. "I think we have agreed collectively based on your actions that this position isn't the best fit for you. Are you sure this is the right fit for you? Your effort and attitude are not in line with our culture or the standards we agreed on."

Leadership is about mentoring people around you and holding them to a higher standard. That means giving them every opportunity to level up before deciding to part ways with someone. It is always more rewarding when someone turns the corner and gets it, but that won't always happen. The only thing you can control is your character and how you show up.

I had the privilege of working with so many amazing people. I made a point to be supportive and compassionate to my employees as we all face challenges both in life and at work. In light of showing respect and patience, our employees knew not to mistake my kindness for weakness. I held everyone accountable to the company's vision and their effort.

Should you be in a position where corrective discipline is necessary, here are some simple steps to follow:

Step 1: Isolate & understand the problem- What is the root of the problem? Is it between 2 people? Is it personal? The first step is isolating and understanding the source of the problem. Often, we try to solve a problem before we understand the full picture and the facts. It might just be a miscommunication or misunderstanding about what is expected or what needs to get done. Isolate whether the problem is comprehensive or compliance-related, then proceed.

Step 2: Find a solution- Can the problem be resolved? What can be done to remove the problem? As a leader, it's up to you to turn problems into opportunities. Your problem-solving solutions should always seek to mentor and provide direction first. Firing people is the easy way out, but it doesn't usually solve the problem. Seek to mentor, explain your desired outcome, point back to your expectations, and find a clear solution to remove the problem.

Step 3: Implement the solution- Create clear guidelines for what has to change. Leave no grey area for interpretation. The goal is for everyone to understand the problem and implement a corrective solution. When problems go unchecked, they only get bigger. As a leader, your goal is to find a solution with the goal of everyone getting back to work. If all parties understand the problem and the solution, that should eliminate the distraction and set the ship back on course.

Step 4: Accountability & follow up- Is the solution working? Have we eliminated the problem? How is it going? Is there a respect in the hierarchy of your organization? This last point is critical. Be accountable to the resolution that you put in place. If there is a disagreement between management and an employee, follow up to see how things are going. Sometimes when you have two great people, you may need to move one person to a different opportunity within the organization so they can grow. This may solve the problem once and for all. You can solve problems permanently by creating new opportunities for the people on your team. The only way to find out if the solution is working, is to follow up and reassess.

Chapter 7

THE MYTH OF SCALE

A common myth in the business world suggests that once you have a great idea, you should create a business plan and immediately start raising capital. You can go that route but let me share why you should wait until you prove your concept and require capital. Let's take Snap Fitness, for example. I could have pitched my idea to investors, but I had no proof of concept that the market actually wanted what I was building. I also didn't want to dilute my company before I got it off the ground.

Instead, I decided to bootstrap the company with my own financing. I built three clubs in all different markets because I wanted to prove that this concept would work in any size community. Even after those 3 locations were successful, I still didn't want to raise outside capital. I had proven my concept and knew it was working, so why would I want to give up equity in my company. I knew that if we could keep up that momentum, we wouldn't need outside capital, and again, I could maintain 100% control of my company.

As a rule of thumb, the less information or proof of validation you have for your business plan, the more equity you can plan to give up. Often the first capital you raise outside of friends and family will likely be the most expensive raise.

Angel round financing groups are typically very sophisticated in the buying process and generally conservative when it comes to evaluating a startup. The stronger your growth, trajectory, and profitability, the higher the valuation will be for your company.

Again, having strong financials, leadership, and fully scalable systems will all lead to higher valuations for your capital raise.

Another route for funding your startup is through traditional financing through a bank. In these cases, you don't have to give up equity; however, most banks will require personal collateral matching your requested loan amount.

The option that I chose was to self-fund my company. I did this because I had the necessary capital in the bank and was not interested in dilution at this early stage of my company. Although the growth or trajectory may be slower out of the gate, the non-dilution of your shares will pay dividends in the long run.

I didn't need to bring in outside investors, which allowed me to maintain 100% of my company as I grew it. Often people seek outside funding because they're conservative or risk-averse. Personally, if you have your own capital and believe in your product, I would wait until you grow your business to a meaningful size and then consider selling a portion to create liquidity for yourself.

Building your company the right way starts with setting the expectation for how long this journey will take. Remember, I spent 20 years in the industry before starting Snap Fitness. The entrepreneurial myth sets a false expectation for how quickly we should grow, scale, and sell our business.

Many entrepreneurs don't fully understand the hill they are about to climb or the commitment, discipline, and sacrifice that journey will require. That's why I believe early on that steady, methodical growth is critical until you feel you have a full understanding of the competitive landscape and the opportunity in front of you. Once you realize that, then you can make a decision based on facts and competitors to determine if you should be raising capital.

I continue to share how long I was in the fitness industry before I started Snap Fitness because many business owners forget to master their category and understand the marketplace. When I sold my first health clubs, I had considered branching out into other categories. However, I was drawn back to focus on the industry in which I had become an expert. We often seek change for variety, but I knew where my expertise was, and I had the discipline to know that I didn't want to start over. My passion was in the fitness and health industry.

When you make the decision to start a business, make sure you are educated and passionate about your category. People often decide to shift industries because they do not see the results as quickly as they would like. Think of these early days as an investment in learning your industry, competition, and pivoting directions as you grow. Remember, success won't happen overnight, and it won't just happen because you raise capital. If you raise capital or scale too early, you can create more problems for yourself. It takes time to hire, train your staff, implement systems and processes to manage a strong growth trajectory.

Set the right expectations and a realistic timeline for how your business will grow. We become disenchanted when we lose track of our progress—set milestones along the way that keep you engaged and help you maintain perspective on your grand vision.

Think long and hard if you're considering shifting industries or deviating from your area of expertise. I've seen it so often where people shift occupations from observations, they've made from other people who make success look easy. The factor they overlooked is the power of passion. Don't shift occupations chasing money. Money is too fast, and you'll never catch it. Find something you are passionate about, and the money will follow.

Dunning Kreuger Effect

I'm sure you've seen this story play out hundreds of times, perhaps in your own life. You find a great idea and get really excited about the pending opportunity. You share the idea with anyone who will listen, and you know this idea is going to change your life forever financially. Then the real work begins.

The lights turn off, and the celebration turns into overwhelm, exhaustion, and defeat. Think of this metaphor like looking at a mountain from a distance. A mile away, the mountain doesn't look so big. It's only once you reach the base, that you realize how difficult your climb will be.

Excitement and anticipation are great qualities because they get you started. But don't make the mistake of early celebration without the perspective of what's ahead of you in your entrepreneurial climb. You have created your vision, but you haven't taken the time to create a plan or start on your progress. What are your goals in the short term and long term? Many of us want to go right into execution but haven't yet created a path with milestones. Once we get started, it's easy to lose momentum and enthusiasm because you didn't know how you would get there in the first place. There was no perspective or plan on the length of time or direction to achieve your goals.

Think about your skills like the metaphor of climbing the mountain. Many of us are attempting to climb that mountain without the proper shoes, climbing gear, and water to survive. You underestimated what you were getting into and lacked the skills to make it to the top of the hill. Our minds naturally want a quick fix solution, but that is simply our lack of perspective. We have watched other people climb the mountain and assume that means we know how to climb it. I see so many young entrepreneurs who think they understand business because they watched a few Shark Tank episodes.

The Dunning Kruger Effect is a psychological phenomenon in which people of the lowest ability in a subject matter and rate themselves as highly most competent, compared to others. Ironically, people who lack the most knowledge on a topic cannot also recognize their own mistakes and errors, making them exceptionally confident and biased self-evaluators. They are also unable to judge other people's performance fairly. Their pride and, at times, ego stands in the way. The best place to start is by acknowledging that you don't know what you don't know. Let go of your pride, ego, and invincibility and commit to learning the skills necessary to climb the hill.

Even if you have a great product with great timing that solves a significant problem, you are likely underestimating how quickly your competitors will shift to copy you. Every time I come into a new market, I evaluate the competition, and more importantly, I figure out how long it will take them to copy what I am doing. Acknowledge that this isn't just about understanding your business. It's also about understanding all of your competitors as well. This is business warfare.

After 20 years of battle, I call the learning and growth stages; I decided to enter the real war. I started Snap Fitness with $300,000, and what I thought was a great idea. Immediately, I needed social proof. I had to validate my idea in the market. I previously shared the early success story. I built the first two clubs in an urban and mid-size market. They were all-cash flowing within 90 days.

The final test was in a small market with 3500 people. I knew that if it worked there, it would work anywhere. Sure, enough, the same results. The club didn't have as many members as a large market, but cash flow was positive in 90 days. The unit-level economics and operating costs were consistent relative to the market size. The real estate and marketing cost was cheaper in the smaller market, and there were fewer competitors. Remember, it's not always best to focus on the revenue you take in the front door. Instead, focus on the profits you take out the back door. As I rolled out the Snap Fitness product, I could see it resonated with what the exercising population was looking for. The dogs were eating the dog food.

At that point, if I wanted to raise capital, I certainly had the performance to do so. I had my systems and processes dialed in. I also had the people in place to handle the companies projected rapid growth. I understood the competitive landscape and knew I had the right product, entering the market at the right time. I had a product that resonated, and my time to market was perfect. There was no need for me to raise capital as I had plenty of interest in the franchise market space; the cash flow was coming in rapidly.

There's a difference between raising capital and creating liquidity.

It was time to run with our concept before competitors had a chance to catch up. Once you validate your concept, it's important to create test environments in diversified market types. Your test environments will provide you with analytics on which markets provide the largest opportunity. Thus, you know which markets are scaling quickest and which markets to enter first. It's important to understand you have a window of opportunity to grab market share with limited competition. That luxury is short-lived, and it's only a matter of time before competitors will try to replicate your model.

The first year I opened 12 locations. By the 5th year, I had invested in human capital, operational standardization, and efficiencies to open more than one location every day. Within seven years of my launch, I had over 1000 locations. Our business model was going up and to the right, and it looked like there was no end in sight. Once you have success and have built momentum, it's tempting to think that success will last forever. Unless you have proprietary technology or a medical product that can't be copied, you will eventually be replicated in the marketplace. Thus, there's a strong possibility your opportunity will be diluted.

At the time, there was another massively successful fitness franchise. I will avoid using the name, but it's important to understand the lesson. In 2005, they had over 10,000 franchise locations. Just six years later, that same concept had less than 3500 locations. This particular franchise model was on fire in the wrong direction.

It is your responsibility to secure a future for your family. There are hundreds of entrepreneurs who have created a concept, grew it to its peak, and then rode it down the other side, selling it for a fraction of its highest value.

Even after expanding to 1000 locations, I was confident that we would continue to grow. Still, I didn't want to regret the possibility that my competitors would take some of our market share. It was time to take some chips off the table.

1. **Taking chips off the table**: When you decide to sell a portion of your business, make sure it's a significant amount of money and understand your competitive risks.

   1. What does the competitive landscape look like?

   2. How easy is my product to replicate?

I realized my company had a valuation of 100+ million dollars. I also knew I was in a very competitive environment. It was time to take some chips off the table without putting any debt against the company. Remember Blockbuster? I didn't want to end up in the wake of a tsunami I didn't see coming. If your industry is very competitive, there will be dilution. Instead of waiting for your competitors to take market share, reward yourself for all of your hard work, and secure your future. I decided to sell 40% of my stock for cash.

This was my life's work, and I knew that if I was going to sell a percentage of the company, it had to be for a significant amount of money. I wanted to make sure that by selling a portion of my company, my trade-off for bringing on partners would be financial independence for the rest of my life.

2. **Maintaining control of your company**- Just because you're selling a portion of your company doesn't mean you must give up control. You can structure your transaction in a number of different ways to create liquidity for yourself while continuing to build, grow, and maintain control of your company. By bringing on partners, though, you must realize you are no longer on your own. You have partners, and you need to be respectful to keep them abreast of any material changes that could affect the company's performance, positive or negative.

3. **Once you sell 51%, it's no longer your company**- In most cases, once you sell 51%, the company is no longer yours. After the second bite of the apple, I gave up control. In my case I sold 40% of my company for $47M and then five years later sold another 20% for approximately the same amount.

I will never forget the day I sold the first % of my company. I immediately thought back to that boy in the two-room school house and my father who moved us to small-town Willmar, Minnesota, because he wanted better for us. I was overcome with emotions because I had spent so many years and sacrificed so much for that moment. It is a moment that will change your life forever. I can't wait to hear about your moment someday.

That's the thing about impossible hills. Once you reach the top of one, you realize that no hill is impossible to climb. It's important to take a moment to reflect on all the work, sacrifice, and lessons you've learned along the way. Once the dust settles, start to pivot towards your next impossible hill. It's time to set your sights higher and climb the next impossible hill.

At this point, I had claimed what I thought was my Impossible Hill. There were no impossible hills because I had the confidence and vision to see it was possible. After a quick moment of reflection and celebration, I created a new North star and followed the hilltaker method again. My financial world would never be the same, but my North star was to build the largest collection of fitness franchises in the world.

I also had partners now that trusted in me. When someone bets on me, I have an obligation to show up for them and perform. And I did. In 5 years, I grew that company 4X. It went from $5 million of annual EBITA (earnings before interest, taxes, and amortization) to 20 million. My investors got in when the company was worth $100 million, and now it was worth $200 million. They got their exit, and they were great partners as they trusted my vision to operate and grow the company.

There comes the point when you owe it to yourself to start a new journey. I had spent over 30 years in the fitness and wellness space. I didn't quite know what I wanted to do with the rest of my life, but I owed it to myself to see what my next impossible hill would be.

When you decide to transition out of your company, I have seen founders make this mistake over and over again. If you are going to sell more than 50% of your company, sell at least 80% no matter what the investors tell you. They may say that you still have a voice in the company, but you are no longer in control. You will always be the company's founder, but it's no longer your company; you're an employee.

It took me took me over 25 years to become an overnight success, and that is the truth about starting your own company. There is no such thing as an overnight success. Success is created by setting huge goals and having a perspective on how long it will take to reach those goals. By the time a company is mainstream, we claim that the founder is an overnight success. However, we don't fully comprehend the years of commitment, sacrifice, and discipline required to make the impossible possible.

Even Amazon, the startup blueprint, took years to fully get off the ground and nearly failed multiple times before it was a mainstream success. Amazon was founded in 1994, and by the time the company went public in 1997, they warned investors to expect "substantial operating losses for the foreseeable future." They had a great idea but were terrified that competitors like Barnes & Noble were catching up.

They started selling clothes in 2002, launched Amazon Prime in 2005, and really exploded by the end of 2009 after acquiring Audible and Zappos, which gave them the overnight shipping and free delivery model which they still have today.

It's critical that you're passionate about any business or occupation you intend to make a career in. It might take years to build a brand and a company that is cash-flow positive. You must be on fire about your vision every morning and commit to the long-term direction of that vision. For some, overnight success might mean a few years. For me, it was 25 years of laser focused effort. That is the hard truth that social media doesn't want you to hear. Social media has created the myth that you can build a successful business with little effort, low risk and high returns. There is a myth of scale and a myth of raising capital that doesn't exist in the real world of business.

Chapter 8

MANAGEABLE CADENCE

Excitement and passion are great qualities to have if you are starting a new venture. I would often have franchisees come to me after buying their first franchise license and say, "I'm going to be your best franchisee, I'm going to own ten of these locations." As much as I love their enthusiasm, the reality is, it's easy to make bold statements without perspective. They haven't started their journey yet and lack perspective on what they are getting into. If they expect to open ten stores, and they only have one successful store, they might even feel like they are failing. No matter what your goals are, set a manageable cadence of consistent continued progress every day.

The franchise owners' excitement slows down once they realize the time and commitment required to build your membership base. Also, there's staff to hire and critical leadership that goes into creating a successful business. Often times, they don't understand the time commitment or the capital they would need to reach 10 locations. They quickly realize that although there is a high potential financial success, it will require work and consistent discipline.

The Snap Fitness franchise offers a turn-key solution, but it's not automated. It requires a lot of work to open a successful club, especially at the beginning. That's why they must follow our well thought out action plan. The first step is to create a vision, the second step is to create the plan, and the third step is execution. In many cases, people underestimate the effort that one needs to put forth to be successful. This is why discipline and accountability work hand-in-hand with progress and perspective. The only way to open ten locations is to open one at a time, through small daily actions and compounded progress.

We all want people in our lives that are inspired and passionate. If you don't have passion and energy, you don't stand a chance. But you also have to understand this is a game of infinite progress, one step at a time and one day at a time.

If you remember the last chapter, we talked about Dunning Kruger effect, where excitement quickly leads to burnout. I want somebody excited to be in the gym for the first time, but I also want to make sure they feel good the next day, not beaten down. If they have never worked out before, let's start by walking a mile. If you feel good tomorrow, bump it up to 1.25 miles. Play the long game of consistency and compounded improvement each day. Preparing for the journey ahead and set a realistic timeline required to reach our goals.

Never forget the timeless lesson of the tortoise and the hare. The tortoise always wins because the tortoise doesn't stop. I want you to be the steady tortoise in your own life. Remember the hilltaker method, one step at a time in the right direction. Most people fail to climb the impossible hills in their life because they lacked confidence or consider past failures they have endured. They assume that this time will end up like all of the previous opportunities.

In many cases, this could be because they lack a realistic perspective of the effort and timeline it will take to succeed, so they quit before they ever reach success. People don't intentionally set out to fail. They fail because they feel the progress is too slow compared to what they thought it would take. Realistically the pace at which they're moving is right on track. They just lack the perspective on where they are at on the journey. The only way to climb that mountain is by putting one foot in front of the other, over and over, and over again. It may sound like a long trail, but it's the only way to build and maintain success.

Think about your business like a skateboard without wheels on a dirt road. You are not going to go anywhere if you jump on the skateboard and start pushing. You start by carrying the skateboard as you walk. After a while, you learn to use your resources, make money, and begin to build your pavement. Eventually, you add wheels to your skateboard and make your first push. That first push is the hardest because you have to create momentum. Eventually, that skateboard builds up steam, and you can jump on to enjoy the ride.

When I was building Snap Fitness, my impossible hill was opening one store every day. That goal wasn't going to happen in the first month or first year. My focus was taking one day at a time while making sure my growth and infrastructure worked hand-in-hand. To reach my goal's capacity and velocity, I had to systemize every small detail in my business. Those action steps might not be fun, but they're necessary.

Every day I created a mindset or process that helped keep me accountable to the material things that helped me grow my business. Often, it's easy for us to get distracted by daily challenges that arise. Over time it can be easy to slip away from your core competency and slip into managing small fires that arise rather than focusing on the big picture. I call that working "in" the business instead of working "on" the business. If you're not careful you can end up running from one fire to the next, eventually losing focus of your core business, which is the catalyst that pushes you forward.

As you grow, be cautious not to focus on expansion until the last store you opened is profitable or strongly trending that way. Often, I get involved with companies that have focused on growth, but in the wake of their expansion, they have struggling locations taking up human and financial capital.

People become overly consumed by growth. But it doesn't matter how many stores you have if they are not making money. Don't compound your problems just because you want to grow. Make sure every store you open is performing and systemized before you open your next. I would rather have one location with 400 members than 3 locations with 250. Remember, when it comes to revenue and profitability, it's not what you bring in the front door; it's what you take out the back.

When my franchisees vision towards success would become clouded or misdirected, I would often bring them back to these four principles:

Step 1: Find People- There was no social media during the early days of Snap Fitness, so we had to rely on guerilla marketing or hand to hand combat to get people in the door. Word of mouth, passing out flyers, member referrals, and our commitment to being part of the community we served. Bottom line, if the people in your trade area don't know about you, they'll never find you.

Step 2: Get them in the door- The first step in winning was getting people through our doors. I knew if we got someone in our door, we had an opportunity to sell them. There was no online enrollment at the time, so we had to get people in the location. Once they came in, there was a strong probability to convert them to a membership. The advertising got them in the door, but it's up to us to sell them.

Step 3: Sell them- Make sure your value proposition is strong, easy to articulate, and relevant to what the customer is looking for. Like all successful companies, you will evolve over time, but early on, our value proposition was five easy points:

1. We were open 24 hours a day.

2. An excellent array of equipment. We had everything you needed to get fit.

3. When you joined one club, you had access to them all. Full reciprocity across all locations.

4. Free fitness and nutrition assessment upon joining

5. No contract; it was on us to earn your business and your trust every day.

Focusing on these five points resonated with our clients, and it was easy for our franchisees to remember. As a business owner, it's critical never to lose sight of what brought the customer to your door in the first place. You must remain diligent to your founding principles and value propositions while always ensuring you're in line with the consumers expectations.

Step 4: Keep them- Selling your customer is one thing; retaining them as a repeat customer requires consistency in everything you do each day. Our non-negotiables provided a clean and friendly atmosphere, the best equipment money could buy, and a community or culture with our members where they knew we genuinely cared about helping them reach their wellness goals.

For someone with big ambitions, I had to exercise patience. My vision was to open Snap Fitness franchises all over the world.

But I also realized that in order for this to happen, I needed to commit to paying attention to the small details early on. It was those basic fundamentals and patience that allowed me to build a global brand. I looked at every new location and each member as one step closer towards my reaching my North star.

Patience is your biggest virtue, but don't use patience as an excuse for your lack of progress. Patience without progress won't get you anywhere. Your goal is to move at a manageable cadence every day, moving towards your goal, but never forgetting that it's thousands of small wins that lead to climbing the impossible hill—give yourself some tools to help you manage your daily tasks to keep yourself accountable. For me, that was creating a to-do list every day. I started making lists when I was 12 years old, and I have done it every day since. It keeps me accountable and provides the discipline to help me reach my daily goals. Remember, it's the sum of small everyday actions that creates big progress.

Part of manageable cadence starts with your attitude. You not only need to have a great attitude; you need to be consistent in your positive attitude each day. If your attitude fluctuates with your business's success, your chances of long-term success will suffer, as will your chances of maintaining a consistent workforce. In most cases, people will only endure so much negative energy from their work environment before they look for their next opportunity. Attitude has a trickle-down effect, starting with you, your management team, your staff, and eventually the customer.

The one thing we all control every day is our attitude, and it's not anyone else's responsibility to make sure we stay positive. That's a mindset that you choose every day getting out of bed. You're going to find when you're positive you're also more approachable. Generally speaking, it's no coincidence as you look at senior roles within an organization; the higher up you go, the more positive the attitudes become.

If you struggle to maintain a positive attitude, here are a couple of practices to consider:

1. Before falling asleep at night and first thing when you wake up in the morning, think of five things you're grateful for.

2. On a Post-it note, write the word attitude in big, bold letters and draw a smiley face. ATTITUDE! Put one of these on your vanity mirror, on your refrigerator, on the dashboard of your car, and on your office computer.

As silly and rudimentary as this may sound, try it, and you will notice a difference.

Consistency with your management style is also critical. You could never tell the difference between my best days and my worst days. That should be your goal as well. Even, steady and consistent. Remember, as a leader, its your job to set non-negotiables and a manageable cadence with your team. How was my staff showing up? Every day I knew that the receptionist at the front desk would be the first impression for every member and potential member.

I credited at least 50% of my first business success to my attitude when I showed up at the club in the morning. I would bring in coffee, ask my staff how things were going, set intentions for the day, and create energy in the building. I wanted my staff to perform at their highest ability, and I know that meant I had to show up on fire each day. This consistency showed them I was engaged with them and appreciated their efforts.

We made sure that when a new potential member came in, we found out their name and made them feel welcomed. Anytime a member came in, we greeted them by name and with a smile. It was my job to light up my staff because I knew creating a company culture each day was the only way we could ever expand.

Consistency and discipline will hold you accountable while moving towards your long-term goals. Set a clear vision and set non-negotiables even on days you don't feel 100%. Some days you wake up full of wind, feeling like Superman, and somedays you feel like Clark Kent. Your discipline and accountability will be tested on those days the most. Every time you feel like quitting or taking those days off, force yourself to show up. Re-enroll yourself into the hilltaker method.

Step 1: Solidify your decision- Once you've made the decision to go for it, decide to go all-in. Don't limp into battle; approach each day as if you are going to battle. Just like a Spartan warrior, be mentally prepared for whatever the day throws at you. You are a hilltaker, and nothing will stand in your way. These are your non-negotiables each day that will get you started.

Step 2: Take one step- There will be days when you feel like progress is at a standstill. Understand there will be days like that, and that's normal. Sometimes progress just simply moves slower than other times. The key is realizing progress is momentum, and as long as you're moving the ball forward, it's a positive day. Take one step towards your North star each day.

Step 3: Bring people with you- Share in the vision, the work, and the profits. I've implemented a cash bonus incentive plan based on efforts and financial goals in every company I've ever owned. These incentives involved every employee, based on their responsibility and salary. Each employee was compensated for their efforts in growing the company. I knew if I ever wanted to reach our companies North star, I had to do it with great people.

Step 4: Set milestones & track progress- It can be difficult to remember how far you've come when your feet are in the fire. While chasing your North star, it's important to set milestones along the way and celebrate those small victories. I remember one of my first milestones being the opening of our tenth location. I had proven to myself that I could visualize the concept, create a plan to succeed, and execute by selling franchises while opening locations. Once it was clear I would launch a successful franchise, I shifted my goal to open 100 locations before eventually raising the number to 1000. From there, my goal shifted to building a worldwide brand. Finally, my goal moved to build one of the largest franchise wellness companies housing several brands under one umbrella. Today Lift Brands holds over 6000+ franchise locations or licenses in 28 countries and growing.

Manageable cadence goes right alongside infinite progress. Many times, people will hit a milestone with their business or weight loss goal, only to celebrate and lose their momentum. Set milestones to show you how far you have come and reward yourself when you hit your goals. Then set new goals, realign with your North star, and keep going. This is the game of life, and it never stops. Remember it's the small decisions and little victories that contribute and allow you to climb your impossible hill.

Chapter 9

EFFECTIVE DOSAGE

Most businesses have a great idea when they get started. They often create some success and then begin diluting themselves and their resources. There will be some days that will be more challenging than others, and you may feel like quitting. It requires mental and emotional fortitude to build a successful business.

Running a business is stressful and not for everyone. There will be days you feel like your world is collapsing, and you may feel disheveled at times. It's important to come back to your foundation. What drives people into your business? Typically, most of your stress is built up in your mind because you are thinking about irrational fears in the future. Your world is not unwinding; it's all in your head. On those days, go back to your foundation and don't allow your irrational thoughts to slow your progress. A lot of those irrational thoughts disappeared when I started Snap Fitness because I was removing clutter from the business. Mental, physical, and emotional clutter.

When I decided to remove the aerobics studio, childcare, racquetball courts, and swimming pools, I knew that I would be losing customers. I knew some parents would go elsewhere because they needed the childcare or enjoyed the aerobics classes. I removed those items because they required a lot of space, had expensive overhead to operate, and only 30% of my members were using those amenities. In my mind, those amenities were not worth the financial or human capital to build and manage.

I realized by not having some of the higher ticket items, I would limit my potential to reach 100% of customers. I knew there would be a trade-off, but the exchange was foregoing some of my sales potential for significantly less upfront capital and overhead. I realized I didn't need to appeal to 100% of the market to be successful. I just had to appeal to 70%. With the Snap Fitness model, I could focus all of my attention on scaling without diluting my focus. I could scale quickly without the mental or physical clutter of building and operating a large fitness club.

My goal was to build a foolproof system and process with a proven model of success that was affordable for any potential franchisee. Why? Because I needed franchisees to help me grow if I was ever going to accomplish my goal. I knew I had to simplify and streamline every aspect of owning a fitness facility if I was ever going to reach 1000 locations. My initial simplifications were:

1. Removing some of the big box health club amenities in exchange for a smaller, more efficient product offering and footprint.

2. The cost of getting into my business was a fraction of a larger full-service facility.

3. Two employees as opposed to 50.

4. Much less startup and monthly overhead, thus reducing the risk exposure dramatically.

Now that I simplified the franchise model to operate, I also removed the barriers that keep most people from buying into a franchise. My goals were:

1. Create a cost-effective model where most people could financially qualify.

2. Streamline & simplify the day to day operations, so you didn't need a wellness background to run a successful club.

3. Reduce operating costs from a full-service facility, making my member breakeven significantly lower and increasing my chances of business success.

We had to make it easy for a franchisee to choose to start a Snap Fitness, instead of starting their own company. We eliminated all of the guesswork of creating systems, processes, and infrastructure that typically comes with starting a business. With our proven model, they could eliminate the pressure of making those difficult and costly decisions.

Remember, hope is not a business plan. Before you ever think of franchising or expanding, you must validate your concept at scale. This is why I built a club in an urban market, a midsize market, and a small market. Before I start accepting peoples hard-earned money as an investment opportunity, I needed to know where the product would thrive. This is part of the reason why I grew my product from an idea to 1000 locations so quickly. I knew that our product was validated and relevant in the marketplace. Franchisees knew it would work in every market, no matter what size. They had the confidence to say yes and open locations with speed.

Create a product that's easy to build, easy to train, making it easy to scale. This is done by continually evaluating, assessing, and refining your entire process. Once completed, create a chronologically defined checklist for accountability on every location worldwide. We have a punch list on how to build out a store, and our franchisees know that if they follow those steps in order, they leave little to chance.

Here are the three types of clutter you should remove so that your business can scale with speed:

Physical Clutter

At Snap Fitness, this meant removing the swimming pools, racquetball courts, aerobics classes, and childcare. That also meant removing old work out machines and creating a stretching area. Don't keep things just to keep them. Look at your business and understand where you have clutter. Remove old equipment, rearrange the room, and simplify your location to make it simple to scale.

Mental Clutter

Do you ever wonder why Mark Zuckerberg wears the same outfit every day? So he doesn't waste time picking out his outfit. You don't have to be as militant about your attire as Mark Zuckerberg, but there is a reason he does it. It's one less thing he needs to think about each day, which frees him up to think more intentionally about the components that materially drive his company and motivate his employees. Save that energy for growing your business.

This was my mindset when creating the systems and processes that went into opening every Snap Fitness location worldwide. Removing mental clutter meant flawless granularity with each task written in chronological order. It also meant including detailed projected costs and timelines to complete. This attention to detail was necessary if I was going to successfully reach my goal of opening one new location every day.

We didn't want franchisees to worry about anything that could slow down the process, and we held their hands through the crucial decisions. Every process was thought out and simplified. Every person that started a Snap Fitness had the mental peace and clarity that they would succeed as long as they followed our process.

Some might ask why such attention to detail, it was important that my franchisees realized and appreciated the time and detail that went into the store opening process. When they saw I had a detailed list of office supplies for the front desk, it gave them a comfort level that I didn't miss anything. They could focus on driving their business through our membership pre-sales strategy.

How can you reduce the mental clutter in your life? What is keeping you up at night? What does your mind worry about constantly?

It's critical that you remove the mental hurdles in your life and create a simplified but intentional to-do list each day. You're going to find that being diligent and disciplined in this thought process will simplify your life and enhance your productivity immensely.

Emotional Clutter

The most important clutter that you should analyze in your own life is the emotional clutter. Emotional clutter will drain your energy and put limits on what you think you can accomplish.

You have heard the saying, "you are the five friends you spend the most time with." That is 100% true.

You have friends and people in your life right now that are not contributing to your growth. Maybe they are outwardly questioning your goals and saying things like, "why would you ever want to do that? or "if you do that, you're going to lose all your money." The people you spend the most time with are either fanning your flame or dousing it. Make sure that you are spending time with people that inspire you to grow and expand.

Removing emotional clutter can be difficult because oftentimes, those people are the people we love the most. I've often wondered why in most cases, it's family members or close friends that dampen your spirits or inject doubt in your dreams. Don't let other people's fear of failure or lack of taking action impact the narrative of your life story. Remember, misery loves company.

It's not that you have to cut friends or family members out of your life. Instead, try to be a beacon of light in their lives and share your excitement and passion for chasing your dream. If they see you living a fulfilled life, it may encourage them to create their own life story with initiatives and timelines. Regardless of their reaction, go back through your hilltaker method and make sure they know why you are working towards your North star. Let them know that you want their support, even if they don't understand you.

At the end of the day, let them be innocent bystanders as they watch you demonstrate discipline and accountability in creating a better life for yourself and your family. Demonstration is the best way to convert others to believe in you. Once they see your commitment and personal growth, they will ask you how you did it.

You can do every step in the hilltaker method, but if you forget to remove obstacles and clutter from your life, your setbacks will be more prevalent. Look at your life and your business, understand what clutter is holding you back, and remove it before you move forward. Leave no stone unturned, take a full inventory of your physical, mental, or emotional baggage, then release it from your mindset. The success and growth you're looking for starts with attitude. We don't want anything holding you back from your full potential or success.

Sometimes, clutter can be disguised by success. I recently became a partner in an acai bowl business that benefited from our streamlining their current business and customer ordering process. It's one thing to remove clutter for yourself, but you may also have to remove clutter for your customers. This particular acai bowl company was no different. We found that allowing our customers to build their own bowl actually slowed down the ordering process, affecting our customer experience. We found that in most cases, our customers were not sure which bowl options blended well together. We created eight signature bowls to combat this inefficiency, each uniquely different from the next, with the perfect balance of taste and variety. By incorporating the change, we not only made the buying experience more pleasurable for our customers, but we also picked up exponential efficiencies in our bowl production.

I initially met the two founders as a consultant to help them evaluate their business and chart a course to grow their business organically. After digging in and streamlining the operations, store build-out, and customer experience, it became clear that this business could be a viable franchise concept. We were able to simplify the business so that it was very easy to operate and simple to explain the value proposition to our franchise prospects.

Originally, they explored the idea of adding kombucha and coffee to the menu to increase profits. It reminded me of our experience with franchisees at Snap Fitness. Our franchisees would often come to us with an idea to incorporate a smoothie shop into our model. I never fault anyone for developing new ideas or wanting to expand their business. However, they didn't think about the costs associated with the expansion.

Smoothies may add revenue to the top line, but once you compare the added costs to the income potential, it proves to be a distraction from the company's original North star. They hadn't thought about the build-out costs to add a smoothie bar, the increased staffing and sanitation, inventory, or upkeep costs to run it successfully.

Along with that, it goes back to discipline. Only a small percentage of your members will buy smoothies and you might need to change the entire business plan to accommodate the smoothie bar. Don't let distractions disguised as opportunities take you off course. Instead, don't be afraid to double or triple down on what is driving your business's core profits. Always navigate back to your North star and pursue your goal with unstoppable fire.

You didn't start this journey to just be comfortable. If you started chasing a big North star, it's probably because you wanted great. Eliminate your fears and ask yourself, what are you truly afraid of? Consider these thoughts on fear:

1. What are you afraid of? Don't confuse fear with apprehension or caution. Our caution can be our best asset because we will be thorough and diligent with our decision-making process.

2. What's the worst that could happen (by removing clutter)? Removing the clutter will help you create your path to making the impossible possible.

3. What's the best possible outcome (once that clutter is removed)? It's important to visualize your North star, but equally as important to create small milestones that can be measured monthly. Progress brings inspiration and motivation.

4. Does my decision align with my North star? Each decision should align with reaching your vision. Vision along with planning and action will be the key ingredient that creates your success.

Your North star navigates all of your decisions. Navigating towards that North star means not chasing clutter disguised as opportunity. It's important you're diligent and intentional with the processes you've created. Once you build those processes, set up your rules to be accountable in your life and in your business. You don't have time for pit stops and wrong turns.

Remain focused on the material components that are the driving force to your reaching your North star. Occasionally in your journey, you may need to pivot because of competition or unforeseen challenges. Trust yourself in the work you've done up to this point. Trust that you're taking the right precautions and thought through your plan of execution with undeniable detail. Don't become distracted or let your dream become watered down or diluted by other people pulling you from your dream. Stay focused on your climb, measure your progress, and inspire everyone around you with your passion.

Chapter 10

HILLTAKERS HONOR

Bill Gates once started a business called Traf-O-Data. Colonel Sanders recipe was rejected over 1000 times before he founded KFC. Henry Fords' first two car companies left him broke, and Walt Disney was fired because "he lacked imagination and had no original ideas." These are just a few iconic brand builders that many might have classified as failures at one point in time. There is honor in playing the game, and failure should be worn as a badge of courage. You really only fail if you stop trying.

I've never quite understood why people are so insecure when it comes to failure. Think of it this way; you haven't failed until you quit. Failing is a natural part of life, and if you are growing, it's virtually impossible not to experience failure hundreds of times throughout your life. The biggest mistake people make when experiencing failure is refusing to look at it as a learning or growing experience.

I often say, "when you fail, fail fast, learn from it and press ahead." I've had the good fortune of having dozens of friends who have accumulated unbelievable wealth and success in their life. All of us have the same sentiment towards success, and every one of us realizes that success is nearly impossible without failures.

The other unfortunate behavior that comes with having a fear of failure is you tend to play it safe in every aspect of your life. This can prove to be detrimental to your success as most opportunities have a limited shelf life. I've seen this countless times where companies have a great idea with huge consumer adoption potential, but they fail to seize the opportunity.

Creating a winning idea or product is really difficult to do. You will need to overcome countless adverse situations as you plow through your road to success. Once you see that glimmer of opportunity, it's so critical that you pounce on it like a lion. This is not the time to play it safe; now is the time to double down with the necessary human and financial capital to seize the opportunity. It's time to gain momentum and take market share.

What would you accomplish in your life if you never let your fear stop you?

I am amazed how often I meet people who have such an unrealistic perspective on what it takes to become successful—both mentally, physically, and financially. I don't know at what point in our society, people got the mindset that they're going to walk into a company and immediately start at a C level position.

Despite what they may have told you in college, in most cases, the real world doesn't work like that. In fact, in most cases, you're going to start at an entry-level position and work your way up through the company's ranks based on the merits of your passion, commitment to excellence, and your ability to lead others.

Your mind is the only thing you can control, and you get to create any narrative you want. Are you a victim who thinks negatively of rejection? If something goes wrong, do you ask yourself, "why does this always happen to me?" or do you pick yourself up and take the hill again?

If you take nothing else away from this book, I would like to give you the gift of turning your failures into success. The gift of creating a muse that will inspire you to get up when you are tired and to keep going after you've failed. Face every opportunity with gratitude and with the understanding that failure is progress. Your attitude towards failure is the only thing holding you back. Why do some people take the word "no" as rejection? While others say "no" is one step closer to a yes.

Earlier in this book, I shared the day my brother and I decided to quit college. We both knew we wanted to be in business for ourselves, although it was probably a fairly reckless decision-making process as I look at it today. It proved to change myself, and my twin brothers life forever.

When I was given the opportunity to turn around a failing health club, my brother and I put our heads together and thought about what would ignite his fire. I love my brother's story because he envisioned himself owning an athletic shoe store, similar to that of a Footlocker. At first, he dreamed of owning one store.

Once he accomplished that goal and the store was profitable, he immediately shifted his focus to opening his second store.

Through this process of continually looking for the next hill, he was able to grow his dream into a national shoe store chain called Athletic Fitters. My brother loved FootLocker and the business of working around athletic shoes, apparel, and active people. Every time we would go to a FootLocker, he would say that he would open up a store just like it.

Our father's grocery store was right across the street, and my dad always warned him to stay away from the big mall. The rent was too high, and it wasn't a good business idea. As you've probably guessed, you can't tell a Taunton that we shouldn't do something or it's impossible because we will do everything in our power to chase our dreams.

My brother took the leap and opened an athletic shoe store in the big mall. He had no retail experience, and we put our cars up as collateral to start his store. His business exploded, and before you knew it, his sales had quadrupled. He was disciplined, and every dollar he earned, he reinvested back into his business.

We watched our father do this for years. We saw first-hand that reinvesting in yourself and your business in the areas of operational and vertical integration would pay huge dividends when executed properly. Our father expanded his grocery store four times. At one point, my father bought a chicken farm so he could produce his own eggs and sell them through his grocery store. That's how committed he was to success and those were the lessons he passed to myself and my brother.

That discipline inspired and instilled the confidence to push my brother into thinking beyond owning just one store, but instead scaling to 104 locations before eventually selling to the company that inspired him, Footlocker. I know what you are thinking, "Peter, success must just run in your family."

Success doesn't run in my family; however, passion, dedication, discipline, accountability, and execution must run in the family.

While he was collecting his life-changing pay day, I was still running that first club making $70K per year. I wasn't struggling, but I must admit how difficult it was to watch my brother and not feel a sense of envy. For me, this would become my inspiration.

Think about how you would feel in this situation. Would you use this as fire in your belly to push you towards success? Or would you say, "well I guess I just wasn't the lucky brother; maybe he will loan me some money?" The story you tell yourself will directly correlate with your results. I wasn't jealous of my brother and given how fiercely competitive we were against each other; I appreciated that he never once rubbed my nose in it. I was fired up because I knew I had what it took to win, and it just wasn't my time yet.

Use your inspiration to get going and fight for what you want in the face of adversity. You may have heard stories of Michael Jordan using his own dark inspiration to fuel his success.

Michael Jordan would create stories in his head about his opponents and use them to fuel him on the court. He passed this mental edge onto Kobe Bryant. Kobe Bryant famously talks about his relationship with his muse when he became the "Black Mamba." This was a mental edge that would allow them both to reach deep, no matter how tired they were, to will themselves to victory.

Michael Jordan didn't stop trying because he couldn't beat the Detroit Pistons. He didn't throw a pity party because they were beating him up. He used this as fuel and motivation to level up his game both on and off the court. He added weight, worked harder, sacrificed to become a better teammate, and use his failures as fuel to win six championships. Michael Jordan didn't win his first championship until 1993. The Bulls drafted him in 1984. Many might have said he would never climb his impossible hill if you just looked at his early career.

When I saw my brother succeed the way he had, I used it as fuel, and nothing would stop me from accomplishing my goals. You can draw inspiration from your critics, even if your biggest critic is yourself. I always kept my father's inspiration and brothers' success top of mind, using it as fuel and proof that hard work works.

Think about the people in your life that have said you couldn't accomplish your goals. Do you believe it, or do you brush it off? Muse or not, I can't stress enough the importance of surrounding yourself with people that fan your flame as opposed to dousing it. Life is unpredictable, and the uncertainty can create doubt in ourselves. Those are perfectly normal emotions that we all have. It's essential to surround ourselves with like-minded people who prop us up in difficult or challenging times. Failure is never final.

At one point, we tried to write our own operating software at Snap Fitness. My development team was confident they could do it, while building the software, we found it cost 3X more than expected, took longer than predicted, and took up far more human and financial resources than it was worth. After several years of frustration, we decided to stop future developments of that software and transitioned to a company whose core competency was developing software. Instead of building it ourselves, we had them cater and customize to meet our needs. Every thriving company has mini-failures and setbacks along the way. The best companies use those setbacks as learning experiences on their journey towards success.

It also led me to look into every process within our company. I did a deep dive and learned early on in my company's history that if I didn't own it, I couldn't control it or set the bar for my customers' experience. This led me to analyze all of our operations from real estate, trucking, construction, payment processing and social media marketing.

Controlling these areas allowed me to keep the pricing competitive while extending warranties and service to benefit my franchisees and our members.

It's challenging to take responsibility for everything that happens in your life. It's difficult to stand up to your critic and say, "you're right, but you won't be right for long." It takes courage to take responsibility for your life and everything in it. It takes courage to admit you have failed and get up to try again.

That is the difference between a hillfaker and a hilltaker. A hillfaker has no control over their future; hillfakers have plenty of excuses and perfectly logical reasons why they can't accomplish their dreams. A hilltaker has all of the same excuses, but they use none of them. They accept the good with the bad. Hilltakers wake up and understand they are in control and they are 100% responsible for how they choose to show up in their life.

At the end of the day, I don't think anyone wakes up intending to fail. The most critical part of winning at anything is believing in yourself. That's where it starts, and that has to be the non-negotiable or cornerstone as to who we are and what defines us. As long as we never stop believing in ourselves, we can turn each failure into a milestone on our journey towards success.

Chapter 11

SERVING SHERPA

So, what is my next impossible hill? I knew I was moving into the next phase of my life, and although I still own 20% of the company I founded, the business is a fully functional machine with capable leadership. The company is far bigger than me. Under the Lift Brands corporate umbrella, we have over 6,000 locations or licenses in over 28 countries.

Throughout my amazing career, I was able to stand on the shoulders of giants who made Snap Fitness and Lift Brands what they are today. I learned at a young age that winning in business is a team sport. It requires hard work, discipline, gratitude, selflessness, grit, determination, and accountability. I watched my dad display these qualities every day he showed up at his Red Owl grocery store.

I always told myself that if I ever made it, I would do everything in my power to pull others up with me along the way. If you have already climbed to the top of your impossible hill, find your next impossible hill to climb, and repeat the process, you must never stop climbing.

Not everyone has the ability to build a financial empire. That's part of the problem in this world. We create jealousy and borders based on the financial success that others may have earned. Consider how dangerous it can be to continuously comparing ourselves to others. That can lead to jealousy and resentment. As you pull back and look at the big picture, if you've lived a life of doing something you enjoy, you have your health, family, and friends; you have a lot to be thankful for. True happiness isn't reflected by a collection of the assets you've been able to accumulate over your lifetime, but rather a collection of your memories, experiences, and how deeply you loved. It's in those things you hopefully find a life full of appreciation and gratitude.

When I decided to step away as the CEO of Snap Fitness, I stepped away from an industry I loved and spent the last 35 years in. Yes, I may have successfully built a fitness empire, but the real gold was the people. I'm most grateful and honored for all the amazing relationships and friendships I made over that time. That doesn't compare to the incredible memories and character-building moments that were dependent on making the right decisions at the right time in a very competitive industry. Some of the fondest memories I have are those moments sitting in my board room with some amazing, talented people as we collectively chartered our way across the unpredictable challenges that come with working in an industry that evolves and pivots at the speed of light.

Although it was a bittersweet decision to leave, I also knew and appreciated what an amazing life I had lived up to this point. I felt compelled to focus on the next 50 years of my life, sharing my stories but more importantly conveying the message, "if I can do it, you can too". I hope that everyone reading this book finds the fire within themselves to chase their impossible hill.

I feel the last 35 years of my life was a grooming process by our heavenly father to put me at this place in my life. I believe my "Why" is to share my real-life experiences with anyone and everyone who aspires to live the American dream. For some reason, one of my gifts provides me the ability to process information very quickly and come up with solutions or alternatives to what can be very challenging times. By hearing my stories, I hope you will inspire your own journey of amazing experiences, wealth, love, happiness, and prosperity.

This book is for those who would like to hear the uncensored version and the truth on what it takes to win both physically, mentally, and financially.

My next impossible hill is to focus on building a platform or forum that allows me to reach thousands of people and provide a beacon of light or inspiration to see their North star and live a life of their dreams. I'm not saying it's going to be easy, but I promise you I will help you create the right mental state to clarify what exactly the journey ahead has in store for you.

These are the lessons I have learned and hope they will help you along the way. If you look for it, doing the right thing will rear its head multiple times throughout the day. It may come in the form of sharing encouraging words or assisting someone struggling with a situation where you have positive historical insight or experience.

Accountability and character reside within each of us. This is the essence of who we are and how we choose to support those around us. Earlier in this book, I spoke about attitude and character. I've always said you can measure the depth of someone's character by the work they do when no one's watching.

There have been countless times when I've been busy in my own life, when I come across someone in need. In all honesty, I feel so blessed and, at times, have such guilt over the life I have. Fortunately, it becomes almost impossible for me to walk past or ignore a situation that could use my assistance.

Knowing this, I do things to prepare myself to react quickly and intentionally without pulling myself away from my own responsibilities. Let me give you an example of how my daughter Sunny came up with a beautiful idea a few years ago that I still do to this day.

A few years ago, my daughter gave me a box with 50 small envelopes for my birthday. Each envelope had a cross and an American flag on it. None of the envelopes were sealed, so naturally, I picked one up and opened it. Inside each envelope, she hand wrote short bible verses for words of encouragement to those in need. Inside each of those envelopes, I added a five-dollar bill; I Carry those envelopes with me everywhere I go.

Here's the beauty; it does as much for me as it does for the person receiving it. Every time I see the envelope, it brings me closer to God. Every time I give one away, I say a short prayer out loud for the recipient in hopes it brings them the courage to press forward and look to God.

When it comes to living life, don't be a bystander. Get in the game, show up early, show up with intention, and show up often.

I remember a quote from the Avengers that really stuck with me. The Avengers were recruiting Spiderman, and when they met Peter Parker, they asked him why he does it? Why does he help people in need?

Peter Parker responded by saying, "When I see people struggling with a problem that I can easily solve, it's my responsibility to help them. If I don't, then I'm responsible for their suffering."

I have spent 35 years building businesses from the ground up. I have climbed the impossible hills you are staring at in your life, and I have prepared myself with the knowledge and abilities to climb those hills. I also started noticing the lies being perpetuated on social media on how easy it is to become successful overnight. Once I saw what was going on, it created a burning desire to share the real truth about success, finding true fulfillment and happiness.

Many people are creating a false belief of real prosperity. The more alarming part is that innocent people are putting their future and their hard-earned money into shortcuts. They believe there are simple hacks to building a life of prosperity. They fail to understand that only a very small percentage of people accomplish the vision they were sold.

There are many truths in this book that are critical components to ensure you have the necessary tools to make your impossible hill possible.

1. Despite what you may have read or heard from some wanna-be business expert, there are no shortcuts to success. Believing this myth will only lead to disappointment and discouragement.

2. As you visualize the goal of reaching your North star, visualize it in its entirety. This will provide you with the motivation and inspiration to hold yourself accountable with great discipline, commitment, sacrifice, and accountability. As difficult as it will be, this will be the adventure of a lifetime for you if you enter this challenge mentally prepared.

3. Nothing is impossible as long as you prepare yourself both physically and mentally. It took me 35 years to get to the peak of my impossible hill. Yes, I had unbelievable moments along the way, and every time I experienced one of those moments, I embraced it with gratitude and appreciation. But I never once settled or compromised on my North star. My drive let me turn my attention back to the ultimate goal I had set for myself, my company, and my employees.

4. Having a positive image and confidence in yourself is the starting point for charting your course towards success. You have to believe that you are capable and deserving of whatever success looks like for you. Otherwise, when things become tough, you might remove yourself from the situation rather than overcome it. You've heard me say it before; winning isn't easy. This is why discipline, commitment, and dedication become so important to press through difficult times.

"Success is where opportunity meets preparation"

Here's an interesting perspective regarding human behavior when what is believed to be impossible becomes possible.

In 1954, there was a belief that it was physically impossible to break a 4-minute mile. Experts warned that anyone who attempted such a feat would die. At the time, it was considered the Holy Grail of sports. Media members and crowds were constantly looking for the superhuman that could break that barrier.

Roger Bannister became the first human to break that barrier, running a sub-4-minute mile. While his accomplishment was a remarkable feat, the real lesson was learned just 46 days later. A man named John Landry ran the mile in 3 minutes 58 seconds. Three more runners broke that 4-minute mile a year later, and all three were competing in the same race.

That says a lot about the word impossible. The truth is that the impossible lives only in our minds. Once our minds believe we can achieve something with the right steps, anything is possible. The other lesson is to be aware of whom you surround yourself with. Three men accomplished the impossible feat of breaking the 4-minute mile, and they all achieved it by competing with one another. I often say anyone can be a hero if you set the bar at your ankles. These men pushed each other to places that humankind had never seen or ever believed could be possible.

Don't ever let someone else's version of what's impossible become your view. It's your life, your dream, and your persistence that will serve you to make your impossible possible.

Who is your Sherpa? Who are you taking your advice from?

The word impossible comes from people who have given up. They use the word impossible because from their perspective, the world around them appears impossible. Unfortunately, people underestimate the power of verbally projecting their shortfalls or defeats onto others. This is why earlier in the book, I spoke extensively on the importance of maintaining a positive attitude. I've concluded that people who tend to have a poor attitude toward life generally have a poor attitude or image of themselves. Remember, your attitude is a mindset and a standard you set for yourself every waking moment of your day.

Most people take advice from the people they love the most. Our impossible hill mindset often comes from parents, siblings, aunts, uncles, teachers, and the people we trust the most. We are conditioned to believe them because they care about us. The problem is that they are projecting the same limiting beliefs that they were taught. Our grandparents grew up without telephones, without televisions, and they didn't have smartphones in their pocket. Even though they love us and want the best for us, they justify their limiting beliefs by saying, "they are trying to protect you."

Oprah Winfrey was an African American woman born into poverty. She was beaten, raped, and abused throughout her childhood before she ran away from home. Oprah grew up during a racially charged time where it was difficult to live a normal life as a black woman, much less become successful. Today Oprah has her OWN television network and is worth an estimated $2.5 billion.

Oprah's story would have been an impossible hill for anyone, except for her.

I want to encourage you to think about your impossible hills and remember who told you that it was impossible. If you are thinking to yourself, "I just don't think I can do it," who sold you those beliefs? Because it wasn't you. Your limiting beliefs were given to you by people that believed they couldn't accomplish their dreams. Those were their thoughts, not yours, and that stops today.

For me, I was blessed to have my father as my Sherpa. He may not have built a multi-international franchise, but he showed me what was possible. I watched him leave everything he knew to move to a small city and take over a failing grocery store. I saw him take that failing grocery store, turn it into a huge success. I watched him renovate and add to the store four times to continue expanding. I saw him accomplish what many people thought was impossible, and he did it by sheer determination, taking the hill every day.

After I saw him accomplish his dreams, how could I not believe that I could fix a failing health club? I believed I could accomplish anything because I had the right Sherpa. Later in life, I watched my twin brother reach his impossible hill. My brother and I were always competitive growing up. He brought the best out of me in many ways and showed me what was possible when he exited his first business.

These were the examples I had in my life and the possibilities I believed in. It was a simpler time when I was growing up. There was no Instagram and far fewer opportunities to feel inadequate. Today, you open your cell phone, and every two seconds, you see photos and videos that will make you feel "less than."

"You are too fat... I have the secret to help you."

"You are too broke... I have the only solution."

"you will never find love... unless you follow my guide."

You are continually being sold that who you are is not good enough. Whether your goals are personal or professional, people become rich by telling you that you can't accomplish your impossible hills. That is the pattern I've watched over and over again. If I'm not careful, even I can fall into that trap if I spend too much time on Instagram.

Just like Roger Bannister or Oprah, your reality is created by your perception of possibility. The interesting thing about perception. All of our perceptions of what is possible are interpretations from previous experiences and encounters. Everything you have ever experienced shapes how you view the phrase impossible.

How many times do you think Steve Jobs was told that putting a personal computer in every human's pocket was impossible? Today we get frustrated if our internet takes an extra second to load.

Once again, everything that has happened and everything that will happen, was once considered impossible.

This is my invitation to fire whomever you are taking advice from in your life and start listening to your heart. There is probably something deep down that you know you want to achieve in your life, and somebody you love will probably tell you not to try. This is my invitation to reignite that fire that lies within you and consider me as your new friend and Sherpa!

There will be times where you will feel your brain start to creep in, saying things like "You're tired, stop," or "you can't do that, why are you trying?" Remember the lessons I've shared in this book and keep taking the next step forward. Let go of the limiting beliefs that were given to you when you were younger. Trust me, I had excellent Sherpas, and even I was called crazy for thinking I could accomplish anything great.

I still remember being that boy who grew up in a 2-room schoolhouse with nothing. I remember what it felt like to watch my dad take the hill every day to provide a better life for our family. I remember waking up and battling every day at my first health club, and occasionally, I would hear the voice in my head calling me crazy.

That's why I am so passionate about the hilltaker method and the concepts in this book. We've been conditioned to believe success comes easy and is for everyone regardless of the sacrifice, discipline, or commitment we're willing to make. We were sold 8-minute abs, 7-minute abs, and then 6-minute abs. If we don't see an immediate result, we lose interest and look for the next shortcut or quick-fix to a million-dollar net worth. People will continue to try and sell you get rich quick strategies as long as you're willing to pay for them.

Here is the secret that they don't want you to know...

THERE IS NO EASY BUTTON, AND THERE ARE NO SHORTCUTS.

At the beginning of the book, that might have sounded a little depressing. You may have thought to yourself, why should I even try?

Now, this advice is liberating because there is no more pressure to accomplish your dreams overnight. Now that you know concepts like infinite progress and manageable cadence, you have the real secret. Stop thinking about the impossible in the short term and start thinking about the possibilities of forever—one step at a time, one day at a time, and one decision at a time. An impossible hill is reached when you keep moving towards your North star and never stop moving.

Taking the hill of your dreams is a lifetime game, so it's critical that you're all in and passionate about what you're doing. Once you find that fire and give your mind permission to believe anything is possible, then you start taking one step at a time towards that impossible hill. There will be road blocks, setbacks, and downfalls along the way, but you're no longer concerned with being an overnight success.

Now you can smile at resistance because it is one step closer to reaching your impossible hill. Now that you have a Sherpa who has given you permission to believe, there truly are no impossible hills in your life.

Chapter 12

TAKE THE HILL

Start to imagine your future self, reaching the top of your impossible hill. Imagine what it will feel like to accomplish your life's biggest goals. Now, start to think about everything you are proud of in your life up until this point. Maybe you were awarded an athletic scholarship, perhaps you fell in love, or maybe you graduated at the top of your class with honors.

If you are honest with yourself, you are likely proud of those accomplishments because they were not easy. The athletic scholarship resulted from years of discipline and hard work, becoming the best athlete that you could. Surely you recall the early morning workouts and sacrificing free time for practice.

If you fell in love, I'm sure you remember the effort you put in each day to grow closer to your partner. You probably recall the deep conversations, the quality time spent, gifts, acts of kindness, and going out of your way to make them feel special. You invested years building trust, growing closer, and developing the love you have today.

If you graduated at the top of your class with honors, you certainly remember the hard work. You remember the late nights in the library, the all-nighters preparing for exams, and the hours spent in front of the mirror, reciting your speeches. You probably missed parties that would have been more fun and may have sacrificed relationships along the way.

Everything you are now the proudest of once seemed like an impossible hill in your life. You were already a hilltaker, and you didn't know it yet. You decided that you were going to be a great athlete, spouse, or student. You swung the first bat, you bought the first flowers, and you aced your first test. You were already a hilltaker, and you took action.

You knew exactly what your vision was, and you probably still remember that vision. You told everyone that you were a baseball player, you glowingly told the world how in love you were, and you said no to after school social hour because you had a big test tomorrow. That entire time, you were solidifying that you were a hilltaker, and your actions were showing others that this was your North star.

You were taking the hill every day, and you didn't even know it. I used those examples for a reason. Most of us find our confidence at a young age, and it becomes part of our identity. We are hilltakers, and we are confident in that area of our lives. We identify ourselves as an athlete, someone who feels loved, or we identify as smart.

Most people stop taking the hill because we are told that whom we thought we were, is no more. Your athletic career ends, and you feel an empty feeling inside; you don't know who you are anymore. That person falls out of love with you, and the relationship ends. You graduate, land your first job, and your boss tells you that you might not be qualified for the promotion. Regardless of which scenario best suits your narrative, it's easy to fall into the mindset of wondering who you are and who you've become.

Our impossible hills continuously change because of what others have told us to believe about ourselves. They are conditioning our beliefs based on their perspective. Even worse, we believe them. We stop taking the hill because we remember that pain of rejection, loss, or our own perceived failure. Most people never take the hill again and spend the rest of their lives wondering what if?

What would you accomplish if fear wasn't in your way?

The only thing keeping you from the hill of your dreams is that fear. Fear of loss. Fear of rejection. Fear of failure. By the end of this book, I hope you understand the myth of fear. Fear never disappears, no matter how successful or wealthy you may become. Fear only grows when you become responsible for hundreds of families' livelihoods with every decision you make.

Your courage just grows a little bigger than your fear each time. Remember, none of your worst days ever killed you, and the only reason you stopped trying is that you were afraid to feel that way again. Instead, what if you converted your mindset to possibility and gave yourself permission to believe in yourself again?

When I started my first health club, I had no idea what I was doing. But I gave myself permission to believe, even though others said I couldn't.

If you ask most people their opinion of Elon Musk, they might tell you he's crazy. He once spent millions of dollars on building an electric-powered car after his dream car exploded. Now, you can see Teslas on every corner, and electric charging stations have become standard.

Elon Musk launched Space X to advance spaceflight with the aim of landing humans on Mars. He's getting closer. He's also launching Neuralink, a brain chip that will solve medical conditions, along with anxiety, addiction, memory loss, and a long list of other issues. He might just do it.

That is the thing about the impossible. Everything is impossible until someone has the courage and belief to make the impossible possible. That is the North star of this book, the belief that anyone can be a hilltaker and that anything is possible.

Thirty years ago, you had to hand-wind your videotapes and drive them back to the store. Now you can watch any movie ever created within minutes on a personal computer that sits in your pocket. You had to track down a phone book, look up a person's name, and hope they were home when you called. Now you can see their face any time, anywhere in the world with the touch of a button. Better yet, a "Hey Siri, facetime dad." Don't even get me started on the impossibility of air pods.

Steve Jobs was another man that decided nothing was impossible. But it's also important to remember that impossible hills are not climbed overnight. Steve Jobs hill started in 1976 when he co-founded Apple with Steve Wozniak. Steve Jobs dreamed of putting a personal computer in the hands of every person in the world. He was perhaps the most extraordinary visionary of our time, and even then, the iPhone wasn't released until 2007.

It took Steve jobs over 40 years to launch the iPhone, and most people stop trying because they are not rich or in great shape after a few months of work. If you believe that anything is possible and the fire to see it come to life, nothing is impossible. Over and over again, we have proven that impossible is a word for the people who have given up.

Before you read this book, you might have been one of those people. None of that was your fault. You have been conditioned your entire life to play it safe, stay in the box, and play by society's rules. They tell you what you can accomplish, and you listen. They say you should be grateful for a job, a 401K, a nice house, and a retirement plan,

They will also tell you that you aren't good enough and you should stop trying. Your friends, family, and own brain may have convinced you that you were a failure because your first business didn't work. They might call you crazy for even attempting what you are hoping to achieve. But now you know, that is actually their belief they are passing onto you. It might be impossible for them, but not for you.

You have been empowered with the truth that anything is possible, but nothing worth achieving is easy. Your North star and big goal won't be easy either. It shouldn't be because nothing worth doing will ever be easy. You won't appreciate easy anyways, and you never have.

You are now a hilltaker that understands this is a game we play forever. There is no shortcut on your journey, climbing the impossible hills of your life. There is no overnight success or get rich quick scheme. There are no funnels that will make you a millionaire and raising capital won't make the climb any easier. You don't need easy anymore because you have a vision and have decided that nothing will stand in your way.

Now you don't have to worry about being an overnight success. You have your entire life ahead of you and a North star to aim at. Solidify your decision by taking the first step. Your climb up the impossible hill happens one step at a time. With each step, you will see yourself getting closer, even when times get hard, or you have setbacks. Setbacks are progress, and every obstacle you overcome creates momentum, confidence, and reaffirms the belief that you will reach the top of the hill.

Remember, you won't have to go it alone. The people closest to you in your life all know your North star and support or at least understand where you are going. You're not worried about the hillfakers anymore. They will be in the same place a year for now when you look back at how far you have come.

You have removed the sandbags and remembered that your courage will always be greater than your fear. You are focused on infinite progress, refining your skills, and getting one step closer each day. You set up disciplines to keep you on track and accountability to follow through. It's the sum of thousands of compounded small decisions that will get you up that hill.

Somewhere on that journey, you will meet the person of your dreams. You will grow into the best version of yourself with every step and every decision you make. Don't forget to stop and celebrate your milestones and progress with gratitude and your supporters along that journey.   Remember, what you are doing is climbing an impossible hill.

Only you know the truth; when you're prepared and determined, there is no such thing as an Impossible Hill!

Made in the USA
Monee, IL
24 July 2021